Upstate D.A.

My time as the
Steuben County Prosecutor
in the 1930s

HON. GEORGE W. PRATT

Upstate D.A.

Copyright © 2024 by Hon. George W. Pratt

All rights reserved.

Published by Red Penguin Books

Bellerose Village, NY

ISBN

Digital 978-1-63777-553-0

Print 978-1-63777-554-7

No part of this book may be reproduced in any form or by any electronic or mechanical means, including information storage and retrieval systems, without written permission from the author, except for the use of brief quotations in a book review.

To the memory of my father, Hon. George W. Pratt, who labored many long hours in recalling and recording his experiences as an Upstate D.A.

Hon. George W. Pratt
1893 - 1971

CONTENTS

Introduction	vii
1. Ambition	1
2. Early 1930s in Upstate New York	2
3. Fulfillment	10
4. Gypsy Mary	15
5. First Trial	18
6. A Guilty Conscience	25
7. A House is Not a Home	35
8. A Case of Rape	39
9. A Shooting	42
10. Brother Versus Brother	55
11. Serious Assault in a Roadhouse	57
12. The Bitch	62
13. The Unwritten Law	68
14. Ring of Fire	75
(Defrauding Insurance Companies through Arson)	
15. Change Of Venue	86
16. Petty Rackets	88
17. Bootlegging	93
18. Fun With The Judge	98
19. Disappearing Evidence	104
20. A Valuable Lesson	111
21. Mob Psychology	115
22. Sneaky Little Tricks Don't Pay	118
23. Parker Murder	121
24. A Coon Out Of Season	129
25. Blackmail	136
26. Hardest Job	141
27. Van Cise Murders Investigation	143

28. **Van Cise Murders** 155
    First And Second Trials
29. **Van Cise Murders** 174
    Third Trial

INTRODUCTION

This book was written by my father, George W. Pratt, who served as district attorney for Steuben County in Upstate New York State from January 1, 1933, to December 31, 1935. He wrote the book near the end of his term as surrogate judge for Steuben County, an elective position he had held for 28 years.

Dad was born in Corning, New York, on June 23, 1893. He was one of six children born to Harry Hayt Pratt and Clarissa Spencer Pratt. His five siblings were his twin sister Sophia, Ransom, Harriet, Hugh, and Helen. The children grew up in a musical environment. Every member of the family played an instrument. And, to the delight of friends and neighbors, the children and their parents used to give Sunday afternoon concerts on the family's front porch.

Playing the violin was very important to Dad. While in high school, he considered being a concert violinist as a career. That dream was shattered, however, by a hunting accident that deprived him of the pinky finger of his left hand. If he were to continue playing the violin, he had to make a choice. Either switch to being a left-handed player so he could use the four fingers of his right hand or continue as a right-handed player but with only three fingers. The latter choice would require special practice and training in shifting positions on the instrument. Dad chose to proceed with only three fingers. He mastered the shifting problems so well that few people ever suspected the handicap underlying his superb performances. For many years, he was concertmaster of the Corning Philharmonic, the local symphony orchestra.

Harry H. Pratt, Dad's father and my paternal grandfather, was the owner and publisher of the *Corning Journal*, a daily newspaper for the city of Corning and its environs, which Harry had inherited from his father, also named George W. Pratt. In addition to his duties as owner and publisher of the *Journal*, Harry served as local postmaster and also served two terms as the local representative to the U.S. Congress.

Dad attended the local public schools, including the public high school, Corning Free Academy, where he participated in the music and sports programs. After high school, Dad went to Colby College in Waterville, Maine, working his way through college by playing the violin in local orchestras for entertainment in various restaurants. He also earned money by teaching the violin.

Graduation photo

CFA Team (author on floor)

Dad must have had enormous energy because, in addition to his paid assignments, according to his college record, he participated in football, track (high jump and pole vault), tennis, chess, bowling, and the senior class committee. He was also the leader of the college orchestra and its solo violinist, an associate editor of *Echo* (the school paper), and the senior class committee. He even gave the parting address at graduation in 1910.

I remember Dad telling me that after he had graduated from Colby, his father had offered to give him the *Corning Journal* for him to make his career as its owner, publisher, and editor. Dad said he would accept the offer only if he could fire the current editor, Eli Mumford, of whom Dad did not approve. Harry said he could not do that because Mumford had been a loyal employee for many years.

Dad, therefore, turned his attention to other pursuits. He began teaching at his high school alma mater, Corning Free Academy, where he taught mathematics and coached football. When Harry was elected to Congress, Dad went to Washington, DC, to serve as his father's secretary. He also enrolled in Georgetown University's Department of Law, attending classes in their night program.

In 1917, when the United States was drawn into World War I, Dad interrupted his legal studies to volunteer as a 2nd Lieutenant in the air reserve of the U. S. Army. He was trained as a fighter pilot in the Army's "Jennie" airplane.

In January 1918, the army ordered him to report to the School of Military Aeronautics at Cornell University in Ithaca, New York, for final training before being sent into combat in France. While he was being processed for transfer to France, someone noticed in his record that he had been a schoolteacher. Immediately, they assigned him to be an instructor of young fliers at Love Field in Texas. Because of the nature of the work, the inexperience of new trainees, and the flimsiness of the Jennie airplane, flight instructors had a higher casualty rate than fighter pilots in combat. There, he remained until discharged in January 1919, when he returned to Georgetown Law School and achieved his LLB degree.

Returning to Corning, Dad started a law practice by forming a law firm with his brother Ransom and an older, established lawyer, William Arland. The firm was known as Arland Pratt and Pratt.

On June 23, 1920 (his 27th birthday), he married his childhood sweetheart, Muriel Addie Cheney, the daughter of County Judge Warren J. Cheney and Addie Benedict Cheney.

Muriel had an older half-brother, Guy W. Cheney, who was a lawyer in Corning and served as district attorney for Steuben County. Muriel had graduated from Corning Free Academy in the same class as Dad and went on to receive a bachelor's degree, followed by a master's degree in Latin at Syracuse University. She taught Latin and English at Corning Free Academy until their first child, Muriel Cheney Pratt, was born on May 25, 1921.

While Dad concentrated on developing his law practice during the 1920s, he and Muriel had two more children, Priscilla Cheney Pratt, on April 25, 1925, and me, George Cheney Pratt, on May 22, 1928.

During this period, Dad threw himself into community and civic activities. A talented and fiery speaker with tireless energy, he joined and became a leader in the First Presbyterian Church, Masonic organization, Lion's Club, American Legion, and Steuben County Bar Association.

As he describes in an early chapter of this book, he was appointed city attorney for the City of Corning. One of his cases required him to defend a city employee against charges brought by District Attorney Guy W. Cheney, his brother-in-law. Dad was always an enthusiastic and energetic trial lawyer, and in this case, which received extensive local publicity, he succeeded.

Mom & Dad

Encouraged by this event, he decided, after considerable reflection, to run in the Republican primary for the office of district attorney—against his own brother-in-law. Steuben County at that time voted heavily Republican, so the real battle was for the primary nomination. Typically, Dad conducted his campaign enthusiastically, and to everyone's surprise, he prevailed as the Republican nominee for district attorney of Steuben County. His success in the general election was a foregone conclusion. He took office on January 1, 1933.

Dad was prematurely gray. By the time he took office as D.A., his hair was entirely white—at the young age of 38. He always felt that the white hair gave him an apparent wisdom and dignity. People assumed he was much older than his real age. Later, he learned that the white hair was a product of pernicious anemia, a disease he had inherited from his mother. Once diagnosed, he followed the prescribed treatment of an injection of vitamin B12 every 21 days plus a teaspoon of hydrochloric acid in a glass of water before every meal. This bizarre treatment, which Dad followed meticulously, kept his anemia under control for the rest of his days.

I do not remember Dad talking about his cases while he was district attorney, but that is not surprising because when he left the office to become surrogate judge, I was only seven years old. I do remember, however, an incident related to the Van Cise double murder case, which is detailed within these pages.

It was Christmastime, and I was selected to deliver a Christmas poem at a children's show presented in the evening to the congregation of our Presbyterian Church. I was on the stage, in the middle of my recitation, when I saw a New York State trooper, in full uniform, enter the sanctuary through the rear door and whisper in Dad's ear. While I continued reciting my poem, Dad immediately rose and left the event with the trooper. I learned later that the trooper had told Dad about an important new clue in the double murder case, and following Dad's policy of personally investigating all such crimes, he had to leave. The story of this murder appears in Chapters 27-29.

In those days, an Upstate district attorney in New York served alone, with no assistants other than one secretary. Many of Dad's experiences over the next three years are described in the book—including murders, arson, and fraud cases. Each one he prepared and tried alone. On December 31, 1935, he resigned as district attorney in order to take the office of surrogate judge of Steuben County, to which he had been elected.

Surrogate judge was a part-time position that also permitted Dad to practice law. He did so, working mainly as a "lawyer's lawyer," trying cases for other lawyers who sought to take advantage of his skills as a trial lawyer. Dad served as surrogate judge for 28 years until he reached the mandatory retirement age of 70 in 1963. He made literally thousands of decisions involving, in total, millions of dollars. In that entire period, the Appellate Division reversed only three of his decisions and modified three others.

Dad's wife and my mother, Muriel, died in 1951. After six years, he married Bessie Philbrick. Upon his retirement, Dad and Bessie sold their home in Corning and moved to a new retirement community in St. Petersburg, Florida. There, he soon was elected president of the homeowners' association, where he led the battles with the developer of the community.

He died unexpectedly on August 24, 1971. He went to the hospital for a routine procedure in the morning. He had an appointment to play golf that afternoon. Unfortunately, he died on the operating table.

I know that Dad was proud of me in all my work as a lawyer. He traveled to Rochester to attend my formal admission to the New York State Bar by the Appellate Division, Fourth Department. Had he lived five years longer, he would have been especially proud of my appointment as a United States district judge. He loved the law and thought that being a lawyer was a fine profession. He would also have been extremely proud that his grandson, George W. Pratt, 3rd, became a lawyer in Utah and that his great-granddaughter, Jessica Wilde, and great-grandson, Eli Pratt, both chose law as a career.

On September 20, 1971, the Steuben County Board of Supervisors passed an "In Memoriam" resolution to be presented to Judge Pratt's family. In that document, they wrote, in part, "He met every challenge of his day and his life was so wonderfully eulogized in an editorial printed in the *Corning Leader* of August 26, 1971, that this Board of Supervisors wishes to have it made a part of this memoriam as a tribute to Judge Pratt's exemplary life. The editorial is as follows:

> *Few Steuben county attorneys have left their work so indelibly written on the records of jurisprudence and politics in this area than did Surrogate Judge George W. Pratt. Few were as colorful and aggressive as the white-maned lawyer whose vitality added strength to whatever pursuit in which he engaged.*

> *Judge Pratt was a fighting district attorney who took a lead in stamping out crime rather than following after-the-fact. He was the key force in the prosecution or investigation of 11 murders during his tenure as prosecutor. He smashed an arson ring threatening the whole county. His short-clipped words and rapid-fire speech gained him the respect of his opponents and the people he prosecuted. He went on to be an outstanding surrogate judge for 28 years.*
>
> *The judge was one versed in athletics because he was an athlete. He was a familiar figure while district attorney—running up and down the football fields of this area as a referee. His white hair belied his age as many an athlete of that day found out, and just as he could control the antics and play on the athletic field, so could he control the attention of an audience before whom he was speaking.*
>
> *He was in demand as a speaker and orator who scorned notes and who could dramatize his points with gestures and machine-gun fire delivery. He was a maverick Republican who added spark to the party, an ardent patriot and dedicated to the teachings of the masonic order in which he reached the highest peaks.*
>
> *Few of today's attorneys remember Judge Pratt as a district attorney or as an orator. A perusal of court records and trials would be enlightening and educational. The challenges to follow would be immense. Surrogate Judge Pratt was a man of many talents who "told it like it was' long before that phrase became today's exhaust for being frank.*
>
> *For Steuben County he was a legend and an edifice in strength. That is why his death on Tuesday seems unreal despite man's obligation to accept the realities of life event at Judge Pratt's 'young' 78.*

With those thoughts, I leave you to enjoy Dad's recollections of the crimes, challenges, and trials of his three years as an Upstate district attorney in the early 1930s.

George C. Pratt
United States Circuit Judge (Ret.)

1
AMBITION

The period of which I write was not a normal time in United States history, nor in the rural, upstate county of Steuben in the early 1930s. It was the unsettled and never-to-be-forgotten period of the last few years of the Prohibition experiment.

Pushed out of the big cities by diligent law-enforcement men such as Thomas E. Dewey, special prosecutor for vice and racket investigations in New York City, organized crime and vice slowly but surely had crept into innocent countrysides. Local lawmen had little experience in coping with such situations. That, in brief, was what was happening in one rural county of Upstate New York when my story begins...

Although I was keenly aware of the inroads that had been made in our county by the criminal element, I had no inkling as to the extent to which they had become entrenched until I was elected district attorney in 1932. Little did I realize that I would soon be journeying to Chicago in the dead of winter in pursuit of an elusive lady "con" artist known as Gypsy Mary. Had I possessed her crystal ball, I might have foreseen a web of double murders, arson, blackmail, and one of the strangest cases in the annals of the history of our county.

2

EARLY 1930S IN UPSTATE NEW YORK

In the early 1930s, it was a far cry from the modern police equipment and methods of the big cities to those of a typical upstate rural county in New York State. The big cities had their police forces operating in concentrated areas, thoroughly trained and drilled in all methods of crime prevention and detection with their special detective, homicide, arson, and riot squads; their bomb, ballistic, and fingerprint experts and files; their two-way high powered radio cars, tear gas equipment, machine and sub-machine guns. In short, the big cities were equipped with the necessary manpower and every possible device needed to cope with the shrewdest brains, tricks, and equipment of the crooks who constantly were trying to beat the law.

Typical rural counties of Upstate New York during that era, which have changed little since then, contained perhaps a small city or two, each having a small police force. The few villages each had a chief of police and occasionally a few extra policemen, with each town having four constables. The county area itself, outside the cities, often consisted of hundreds of square miles of territory and had only a sheriff, an under-sheriff, and a few deputy sheriffs, mostly without any prior police experience. Most deputies were usually appointed because of the political influence they had.

In addition, the New York State Police, with a substation or two having a squad of from four to eight troopers in a county, separately covered the areas outside of city limits and were available to assist the cities when requested. Naturally, in the course of their investigations, they worked in every rural part of the county and frequently within the cities themselves. The paths of the State Police, Sheriff's force, and City and Village Police frequently crossed; oftentimes, too, they worked together on the same cases.

The State Police, the City Police, and a small few of the Village Police were "career men"; they had chosen police work for their life work—they studied methods, attended police schools, and so far as possible, with limited equipment tried to make life tough for all law violators. Contrary to popular opinion, they were then and still are, by and large, a fine, loyal, intelligent, hardworking small band of men, ready to risk their lives on an instant's notice and eager to work on cases that were outside of the usual routine.

The sheriff, being an elected official, necessarily a politician, and many times without any prior police experience whatsoever, usually selected his deputies to pay political obligations or with the idea of perpetuating himself in office. Fortunate was the sheriff who was able to acquire one real "cop" on his staff; if he got two, it was almost unprecedented.

Sheriffs and their deputies were usually conscientious, oftentimes ambitious to do a real job of law enforcement. Upon taking office, they read and studied some of the standard works on crime detection and, in their simple way, tried to justify the confidence of the people who elected the sheriffs or of the party leaders who jammed them down the throats of the electorate.

On the whole, sheriffs and their staffs ran the jails efficiently and competently and looked after civil business, handled highway patrols and routine small complaints, usually with dispatch and diplomacy. But, when a major crime broke, there were few sheriffs' staff equipped to tackle it. They lacked the training, experience, ability, and modern police technical equipment.

Constables of the towns were either elected by the voters or appointed by the town boards. Their duties were largely serving civil papers and keeping order by making small arrests for drunkenness, disorderly conduct, petit larceny, and the like. However, quite often, they were of inestimable assistance when a major crime occurred because of their intimate knowledge of the townspeople, their immediate territory, and the local conditions.

The railroads maintained a small staff of trained police officers who, in addition to their own specialized problems connected with railroad protection, were very helpful to the police and prosecutors. On the whole, these railroad officers were good "cops," diplomatic, yet tough when occasion required, and they furnished much valuable information to other police authorities.

One of the biggest drawbacks in the past had been the unfortunate petty jealousies that occasionally arose between some of the various police organizations, especially between sheriff's departments and the State Police. There was a neutral rivalry existing between the two. Unfortunately, some of the State Police, being "career men" with the advantage of superior training and a more comprehensive and much better-equipped organization, resented the efforts of sheriff's departments, which they generally considered amateur organizations.

The sheriffs' departments, on the other hand, trying conscientiously to do their jobs and having more or less an inferiority complex, resented the superior efficiency and attitude of the State Police. Law enforcement, in general, therefore, was the loser.

In some instances, when one group obtained some valuable evidence, which should have demanded cooperative sharing and work, it did not pass such information on to the other group but kept it secret. The other group, therefore, would sometimes waste hours, days, and even weeks trying to acquire such evidence that was already known to the first group. This was an intolerable condition, and it caused many a heartache to a prosecutor who was trying to build up the best possible case.

In the big cities in New York State, the district attorney was largely an executive. He had a number of assistants, clerks, and trained investigators, either on his own staff or assigned from the city police department. The prosecution of crimes was left largely to the assistants. Each assistant district attorney specialized in a particular type of crime, such as homicide, sex, robbery, crimes of violence, larceny, and fraud, or in drawing indictments, doing appeal work or preparing cases for grand juries.

Several of the assistant district attorneys were trial specialists or functioned under other special classifications of criminal law. Their offices were near the center of their court work; they had all the facilities of the police—fine libraries, morgues, medical examiners, pathologists, autopsy specialists, and laboratory specialists—and had available for consultation and expert use, the best and most experienced medical, psychological, and psychiatric talents that the city and state hospitals afforded. And the medical, technical, and mental experts in the big city and state hospitals and the laboratories of New York State were and still are the peers of any in the world.

The city police were closely associated with the D.A. They cooperated with him in every possible way, running down every clue, rounding up every possible person for questioning, using informers or "stool pigeons" and other possible contacts within and without the underworld. They assembled and analyzed evidence to help make ironclad cases for the prosecutor.

In most of the rural counties, however, the D.A. had no assistant. He did all the work alone. He secured the evidence from the police authorities, interviewed all witnesses, took statements, took photos, made maps and sketches of the scene of a crime or directed and supervised such work, attended preliminary examinations in magistrates' courts, prepared the cases for grand juries, and opposed motions which sought to reduce bail, to inspect grand jury minutes, or to secure release on Habeas Corpus of prisoners who were confined.

Also, the district attorney argued appeals from convictions for felonies or from Magistrates Courts, made cases ready for trial, looked up the law, made trial briefs, and attended to gathering witnesses. He arranged for examinations by experts if insanity was a defense or if questions of handwriting or of ballistics or other technical matters were involved. The D.A. crammed up on whatever medical features might be coming up in a trial, attended to the arraignment of prisoners, investigated and passed on bail bonds, and presented cases to the grand jury. He also was the only one who tried petit cases in Magistrates Court, indictable misdemeanors and felony cases in County Court, and murder cases in Supreme Court. And he tried all cases himself, although many times he was opposed by two or more wily defense counsel.

Typically, a D.A. was allowed a clerk at a nominal salary, usually not exceeding $15.00 per week in upstate counties. And the D.A. did all this on a magnificent salary of from $1,500-$5,000; in the writer's case, it was $3,600 for the first year and $4,800 for his next two years.

The only real assistance the Upstate D.A. got was from the police authorities who worked on the cases. Their work had to be carefully reviewed and reorganized so that the evidence would not only be legal, but logical and not subject to objection or rejection when presented in court.

The only experts available to the writer during the three years of 1932, 1933 and 1935 were the director of the Steuben County Laboratory or one hired from outside the county for some special purpose like handwriting, insanity, ballistics, or the like.

More recently, however, with the development of the Bureau of Criminal Investigations of the New York State Police, very competent plain-clothes investigators and technical experts in all fields of criminology, including handwriting, typewriting, and fingerprinting, auto tire identification, ballistics, microscopic, physical and chemical examinations of blood, paint, cloth, wood, metals, twine, hair, skin, and many others, have become available to all counties. But in the early thirties, each sheriff's office had to do all these things alone unless the D.A. called in, at county expense, recognized experts in those fields.

Add to this assortment of duties and responsibilities of the D.A.'s and sheriff's offices the fact that most of the jury lists in rural counties, both grand and petit, were not selected by jury commissioners who had carefully made up their jury lists after personal examination and further outside investigation of the prospective jurors. Jurors were selected in the antiquated, political manner of our forefathers by having the town and city supervisors and assessors collaborate and make up a jury list from their town, city, or supervisor's district. The result being that personal friends or political henchmen of the selectors were chosen regardless of their mental makeup or moral stamina. Jurors then were all males. Females were not permitted as jurors in New York State until 1937.

Such a typical upstate rural area was and still is the County of Steuben. Situated in the western, southern tier of New York State, it is the fifth largest county in the state in area, larger in area than the state of Rhode Island. In 1932, it had a population of about 84,000. Of that, about 16,000 were in the city of Corning, with its surrounding villages of Painted Post, Riverside, South Corning, and the hamlet of Gibson having 4,000. Sixteen thousand were in the other city, Hornell, with about 4,000 more in the villages of North Hornell and Arkport. The other 44,000 people were scattered in typical farming villages and rural areas. It was all connected by 3,200 miles of roads.

Corning then had three railroads, the Erie, the Tioga Division of New York Central, and the Delaware, Lackawanna & Western. The New York Central had a fairly large railroad yard, the Erie a smaller one. Its principal industry was and still is Corning Glass Works, the world's largest manufacturer of technical glass, with Ingersoll Rand having a large plant for manufacturing compressed air machinery at nearby Painted Post.

Hornell had a large Erie railroad yard and engine and car repair shops and was largely a railroad town with several silk mills of considerable size. The village of Hammondsport, on beautiful Lake Keuka, had four or five large wine cellars and wineries both before and since Prohibition. Wine and champagne making was, and is now, a major industry in the environs of Keuka Lake.

Although there are courthouses in Corning, Hornell, and Bath, Bath Village was the county seat. Bath was a quaint, picturesque village of about 4,500 and, besides the County government, had a ladder manufacturing plant and a United States Veterans Facility with a capacity for about 1,500 veterans, including a very modern 200-bed hospital. The population of Steuben County was mostly of English stock, with a mixture of many fine families of Irish, German, Dutch, French, Swedish, Norwegian, Italian, and Polish descent.

The countryside was largely rolling, forest-covered hills, some of which were mountainous in size, with a few very fertile green valleys. Farming was chiefly of potatoes, hay, grain, corn, grapes, buckwheat, and beans, with extensive dairy operations. People, on the whole, were "God-fearing," intelligent, and "law-abiding." Many of them, however, were hard-pressed in trying to make a living, particularly during the years of the Great Depression. In both the back rural areas and the cities were a few isolated examples of low moral conditions and wretched standards of living, which put the slums of the larger cities to shame, unbelievable as this seems.

Steuben County in the early thirties had a total of about seventy-five churches, while the little red schoolhouses of the rural areas were rapidly being absorbed into Central School Districts.

The period of which I write, however, was not a normal period in United States history. It was the unsettled and never-to-be-forgotten period of the last few years of our country's prohibition experiment. All the evils of Prohibition were in full flower. Al Capone, Dutch

Schultz, Waxey Gordon, and thousands of lesser liquor barons ruled the underworld.

J. Edgar Hoover, our top-flight G-Man was just beginning to develop his organization into its present state of efficiency. When the kids played cops and robbers, all the kids wanted to be John Dillinger or some other famous gangster. In some of the upstate cities, like Buffalo, Syracuse, and Rochester, police had made life miserable for some of the would-be "big shot" small-time gangsters and racketeers, and these "rats" sought safety in the greener and more innocent pastures of rural New York State.

Road houses sprang up, easily accessible by car from centers of population. Some of them were just "pigs ears" where a poor quality of "white mule" liquor was sold at top price. Others had rooms for philandering couples and offered girls for rent.

Organized crime and vice slowly but surely had crept into these innocent countrysides, and local sheriffs' outfits had little experience in coping with such situations. New York State had no special enforcement law to supplement the Federal Volstead Liquor Act, and Federal agents were too few and far between to cover the vast rural areas of Upstate New York. The Federal Prohibition Act was tricky, and there was a woeful lack of enthusiasm for its enforcement.

Much of Steuben County had been dry through local option before prohibition. At that time, the Women's Christian Temperance Union was a group to be reckoned with in this Republican-leaning area.

In brief, that's a thumbnail sketch of this typically rural county of Upstate New York in the early 1930s, as it was when my story begins...

3
FULFILLMENT

It was with such a background of times and conditions that I decided I should like to become district attorney of the county of Steuben, in which I had been born and raised. After practicing law for eight years in the city of Corning, I was appointed city attorney. One of the duties of the city attorney was to appear in City Court for the Police Department on contested traffic violations and all minor crimes that were being prosecuted by the city police.

At that time, Corning was infested with a number of bootleggers, and the city police were having difficulties in trying to keep them in line through disorderly conduct charges, there being no state law requiring enforcement against liquor violations. Local bootleggers seemed to have little difficulty in evading the prohibition enforcement officers of the Federal government and took great delight in their game. As city attorney, I was also kept reasonably busy in assisting Corning City Police in their attempt to keep petty crime at a minimum.

In addition to those matters, the chief of Corning City Police brought charges, which I successfully prosecuted before the police commission, against one of the local policemen for a number of counts of dereliction of duty. The accused policeman, Raymond Brooder, retained as counsel to defend him the district attorney of the county, Guy W. Cheney, who incidentally was my brother-in-law. In many ways, Guy was a crack prosecutor and a very able trial lawyer. The hearings on these charges attracted widespread public attention, and the case was fiercely and bitterly contested.

Although I had never defended a criminal case, I had had considerable trial experience in civil matters in courts of Justice of the Peace, County Court and Supreme Court. But this prosecuting experience as city attorney had rather fired up my ambition to continue further along this line. So, I asked my brother-in-law when he would be retiring, as he had been a prosecutor for about eight years at that time.

He requested that I hold off running for district attorney for a while; he wanted one more term of three years, and then he said he would retire and support me as his successor. With this in mind, I continued my growing trial practice until January of 1931, which was the year that his new term was coming to an end. I again approached him about retirement and supporting me. but he wanted me to wait for another three years.

In the meantime, he had been assigned the prosecution of a very unpopular murder case in which the sympathies of the community were pretty much on the side of the accused. In the handling and trial of that case, he had come in for considerable criticism all over the county. The jury had found the defendant not guilty after a very bitter, hard-fought, and expensive trial, and public opinion, perhaps unjustifiably so, disapproved of the way he handled the case.

Son of a county judge, my brother-in-law was well known to the people of Steuben County, not only because of his work as a prosecutor but because he had been secretary of the Republican County Committee for a number of years and also a member of its executive committee. For the most part, therefore, he had the backing of the Republican County Organization.

Guy also had been an attorney for a number of towns in the

county, had been an active trial lawyer in civil matters, and was a member of the Boards of Education of one of Corning's two city school districts. He had also been the past exalted ruler of the Elks, a member and past president of the Rotary Club, and active in other civic and fraternal organizations. He was a public speaker of note and had enjoyed audiences in the two larger cities and all of the villages and towns of the county on interesting topics.

Yet, I was just young and brash enough at thirty-eight to think that I might be able to capitalize on the unpopularity of the Lawrence Guiney murder case and some other lesser mistakes that Guy Cheney had unwittingly made as district attorney.

At first, the politicians, except the chairman of the Republican County Committee for whom I had done a political favor, while personally very friendly, rather regarded my candidacy as a joke. With two exceptions, so did the editors of the various newspapers of the county. One of the exceptions was the editor of a country newspaper in the village of Canisteo, who, afterward, became the Republican county chairman. For some reason unknown to me, he didn't care much for my brother-in-law. The other editor was a warm personal friend.

So, with the help of my father, an old-time politician who had served two terms in Congress and knew how to carry on a political campaign from all angles through hard personal campaigning, I was soon able to create considerable interest in my campaign.

I found that in most towns, there were usually at least two factions, one of which was a predominant organization and the other being more or less the discontented faction. In most of the towns where the organization predominated, I was able to get the discontented ones on my side and induce them to put candidates opposing the organization candidates in the field for supervisor, town superintendent of highways, justice of the peace, or other local town offices. To some extent, I helped them with their campaigns in exchange for which they helped me with mine.

If there were no apparent controversies brewing in a town, I proceeded to stir up controversy and get candidates to enter the field against the organization's candidates. In a few of the towns, I finally won the organization over to my side. Through personal campaigning in small groups and with the help of a few well-known professional and business people of the county who would introduce and sponsor me to people of the towns and villages and in the cities, I gradually acquired considerable support.

Then, capitalizing on a final vigorous and rather spectacular advertising campaign, which pointed out the tremendous expense of the unfortunate Guiney murder case and some of the things that we charged were a mishandling of that and other cases, the interest in the campaign became rather intense as primary day approached.

In the meantime, a third candidate, Lyle W. Jackson, entered the field; a rather popular, easy-going lawyer from Hornell, New York. He hoped to capitalize on the rather bitter fight that was ongoing in our end of the county and get votes in his own end of the county and thereby squeeze in. But, we recalled the presidential campaigns of Woodrow Wilson, Theodore Roosevelt, and William Howard Taft in 1912 when Teddy and Wilson lambasted each other, and everybody forgot Taft. My brother-in-law and I lambasted each other as to our respective records and qualifications. Nobody said anything about Attorney Jackson, the third candidate, and he became the forgotten man, just as Taft was in 1912.

A few days before the primary election, the newspapers wanted statements from the candidates as to their predictions about the final result. The newspaper writers had conducted surveys and predicted that the number of votes in the Republican primary would be between eight and nine thousand. Both Jackson and Cheney gave glowing predictions of how they would each win, but I refused to give any prediction at that time. I did tell them, however, that the vote would be between twelve and thirteen thousand, but they rather ridiculed the idea, both personally and in their papers.

My father and I, however, had made up a prediction for ourselves, analyzing each of the 72 election districts in the county and showing that I would win by more than 500 votes. We sealed this prediction and locked it in my safe until primary night, and after the votes were counted, we were only off by 200. We had given Jackson 200 votes too many in his home city of Horne, which I had picked up. Otherwise, the districts ran almost as we had laid them out; there were nearly 13,000 votes cast, and I won by more than 700 votes.

This primary upset was not only a surprise but a shock to a great many of the County politicians and political writers, but it didn't take them long to extend the olive branch to me, and from that time on, for many years, I had no trouble politically. As this county was better than two-to-one Republican, there was no trouble in being elected on election day, Tuesday, November 3, 1931.

4
GYPSY MARY

During the late spring or early summer of 1931, while the primary campaign was going on, some Gypsies came to the city of Corning and rented a small place on upper West Market Street, the main thoroughfare, where, among other things, they were engaged in fortune telling and phrenology. Although the local police had them under surveillance, one of the Gypsies, a woman called "Gypsy Mary," whose name was Mary Stevens, whom we afterward found out was one of the slickest articles in the business of fleecing the unwary, made friends with one of the local glass workers by the name of McMahon.

They became romantic and in addition to telling his fortune, she wormed from him the fact he had some money saved up. After inducing him to bring it to her fortune-telling parlor, where she and her gang were operating, she convinced him that she could double or triple that money within a very brief period of time by certain rites known only to Gypsies.

Taking his more than $2,600 from him right in plain sight, she mumbled some mumbo-jumbo, a sort of incantation supposed to be mystic words, and performed some weird passes of the hands over the money. She told him she was blessing it in the Gypsy language and did it up into a roll, which she carefully wrapped and put in a small sack and then tied up the sack with a ribbon. Hanging this sack around his neck, she told him to keep it inside of his clothes, even his night clothes, for three days and then to come back. She would open it with proper Gypsy rites and the money would be mysteriously increased, perhaps doubled or even tripled in size.

Under no consideration was he to open it, as it would destroy the spell.

Simpleton as he may seem, he did just that, trustingly waiting the three days. When he returned to the dingy shop, he discovered the Gypsies had flown. He opened the sack and found less than $10 in one-dollar bills wrapped around rolls of paper. With great indignation, he complained to the local Corning city police, who did everything possible to trace these Gypsies.

The city's finest patrolman, William P. Jones, who also doubled as a detective, was assigned to the case. A warrant for grand larceny was obtained out of Corning City Court, and as soon as the grand jury met, the district attorney obtained an indictment.

The usual police notifications on "flimsies" were sent to various police and sheriff organizations throughout the eastern United States, but nothing more was heard until Christmastime 1931, just before I was to take office. We were notified that Gypsy Mary had been located in Chicago. A warrant was issued whereby she was to be arrested and extradited to Steuben County for arraignment and trial.

Immediately, she secured a writ of habeas corpus in the proper court in Chicago. It was returnable on January 2, 1932, the day after I was to take office.

The day before New Year's, I went by train to Chicago, where I was cordially received by the State's Attorney's office, and one of their specialists in this matter was assigned to this case to oppose the writ. Gypsy Mary was defended by a well-known Chicago attorney, who in the State's Attorney's office was called "Habeas Corpus Anderson."

After a rather brief but sharp hearing before a judge in the Criminal Courts Building in Chicago, the writ was thrown out, and Gypsy Mary was remanded to our custody. But Anderson had an appeal all ready with a bail bond, which he immediately proceeded to have approved.

I rather questioned the sureties on the bail bond, but the State's Attorney's office assured me that their bail bond department had investigated the real estate that had been put up as security. Before we could get her out of the building, Habeas Corpus Anderson secured a stay on the basis of the appeal and the bail bond, and Gypsy Mary was released from custody and promptly disappeared.

We thereupon tried to recover the bail but found it was a vacant lot in the depths of Lake Michigan. I returned to Steuben County a disappointed but wiser man.

Later, we learned that Gypsy Mary had been picked up again in Philadelphia. I sent an officer with a governor's warrant, and he met with almost the same treatment that we had received out in Chicago two years before. At the hearing in Philadelphia, the officer reported back that the King of the Gypsies had taken him quietly out in the hall and offered him $3,000 if he would head for home and forget about this. But that didn't prove to be necessary; with other legal maneuvers, they were again able to obtain her release on bail and again spirit her out of the building before we could take her into custody. We never succeeded in locating her again.

Our investigation showed that she certainly was one of the slickest con artists in the business. Apparently, she was wanted all over the United States, but nobody seemed to be able to hang on to her very long. The Gypsies were apparently willing and able to put up all kinds of money to keep her out of jail and keep her in active circulation. She was a great source of revenue for them.

5
FIRST TRIAL

On June 14th, 1931, while our political campaign was still raging, three Addison men, Theodore Laffkas, Edwin D. Curtis, and Harry Fritts, driving through the town of Cameron, saw a barn burst into flames, and a car speed out of the barn's driveway. There were indications of "great hurry" as the car tumbled onto the main highway.

One of the three Addison men noted the license number and wrote it in the dust on the dashboard with his finger. Afterward, he transferred it to a card. They summoned the authorities and neighbors and tried to put the fire out themselves. The barn was a total loss, and a nearby house had also caught fire but was extinguished.

Working in Steuben County at that time and for a number of years thereafter was a dedicated officer, Sergeant Charles G. Burnett, who was in charge of one of the outposts of the State Police. The men from Addison reported to him and to the justice of the peace of the town, Francis Jackson, what they had seen, and also that they had found oily rags and waste material in the barn and at the house, indicating the possibility of arson.

Sergeant Burnett and his troopers investigated the matter thoroughly, but my brother-in-law, District Attorney Cheney, didn't think they had enough evidence for an indictment. The Sarge, however, was a bulldog, and once he was convinced that a crime had been committed, he never gave up. He finally secured a little more evidence and found out that the driver of that car was one Robley Chapman and that the house and barn were owned by one Pearl VanDewater. She was away at the time of the fire, and thereafter, she had put in a claim to the Hartford Insurance Company for damages on her two properties.

After I was elected, Burnett laid the case before me. We put it in before my first Grand Jury and secured an indictment against Pearl VanDewater on two counts of arson second degree and arson third degree for burning the barn in violation of Sections 222 and 223 of the Penal Law of the State of New York. These sections of the Penal Law carried very stiff penalties for someone found guilty.

Pearl VanDewater was duly arrested and arraigned. She pleaded not guilty and was represented by Floyd Whiteman and Vido M. Candiello of Hornell. Whiteman, although blind, was one of the outstanding trial lawyers in the state, and he had one of the most remarkable memories of any lawyer in this area. After two or three days of trial, some question came up as to what a witness had testified to several days earlier. He quoted the testimony verbatim, question and answer, and I quickly learned not to challenge any of his statements about testimony. He was always right.

In the city of Hornell, there was a brilliant newspaper correspondent by the name of Ellis Knapp representing several morning papers, which had considerable circulation in and about Steuben County, particularly in Hornell. He became much interested in this case, and scenting news value in taking the side of the defense and playing up the heavy penalties for arson, he squeezed every ounce of news out of the events of the indictment, arraignment, and trial. This, in effect, was potent defense propaganda.

At trial, the case was entirely a circumstantial evidence case. Juries don't like such cases, although such evidence can be far more reliable than direct evidence. They are not subject to lapses of memory, prejudices, personalities, frailties, or imaginations of witnesses.

Sergeant Burnett had the help of a representative of the arson department of the National Board of Fire Underwriters, a special agent named Grover C. Darrow, who had headquarters in Rochester, New York. Our main witness at the start of the case, of course, was Sergeant Burnett, who linked together all the various elements that we had assembled, pointing unerringly to the fact that the defendant had had this barn burned by this young Robley Chapman for the sole purpose of collecting on the insurance.

Defense Attorney Whiteman, at all times, kept the jury conscious of the fact that he was blind. He would stumble around and feel his way along the counsel table and the bar separating the jury box, where he would take out his watch and open the case with trembling fingers, put his fingers on the hands and dial to see what time it was and carefully restore it to his pocket. In that subtle way, he attempted to obtain sympathy for his client through sympathy for his handicap.

Defense attorneys always plan to try everybody connected with the case except their defendant client. First, the prosecutor, then the police. Then, all prosecution witnesses, and if this does not seem to be enough, they then turn on the judge, making repeated motions for mistrial on the grounds of unfairness to their client. I have even seen them try the jury in desperate cases.

As a cross-examiner, Whiteman was without peer in our county. In an endeavor to break the chain of circumstantial evidence and get the jury's mind away from his client and her connection with the crime, he went after Sergeant Burnett with a vengeance.

He accused the State Police, and Burnett in particular, of persecuting the poor, honest people of this county, of hounding them not only on traffic violations but on other petty matters, of parading their uniforms and revolvers before the public. He even accused them of competing against the number of arrests made by the sheriff, thereby fomenting discord in rural areas for the purpose of aggrandizing the actions and usefulness of the State Police and making charges and arrests in order to build up the State Police total.

Whiteman attempted to turn the trial into a trial of Sergeant Burnett and the state troopers over whom he had command in this county. He made some headway, but the judge sustained numerous objections and warned the defense attorney time and again against using such tactics. Whiteman then turned on the court itself. He accused the court of not giving the defendant a fair trial and made motions for a mistrial on the grounds of prejudice. In fact, he did about everything possible to create an atmosphere of unfairness and prejudice. This was headlined and played up in the newspapers by correspondent Knapp.

After the third day, Sergeant Burnett got me off to one side before court started and said that the night before, he had gone to the home of this Robley Chapman on information that had been furnished to him and found that Chapman had in his possession a revolver without a permit, which was a violation of Section 1897 of the Penal Law.

I immediately sent for Chapman and put it to him cold turkey that he was going to be arrested for this violation, and the consideration that he would get from me would depend upon whether or not he would go on the witness stand, turn state's evidence, and tell the truth about this whole matter. Chapman then broke down and confessed that the affair had happened just as our circumstantial evidence had indicated. He told us that Mrs. VanDewater had hired him to set this fire when she was to be away, that he was the one who had prepared the incendiary device, touched it off, and dashed out of the driveway in his car just as the witnesses Curtis, Laffkas, and Fritts had testified.

When Court opened that morning, I immediately put Robley Chapman on the stand whereupon he spoke in detail about the plot to burn the barn for the $500 insurance money (of which he was to get $100) and to set fire to the house in order to distract attention so that the barn would be a complete loss. It didn't appear that he ever seriously intended to demolish the house, and, in fact, that's exactly what happened.

It was obvious the jury was intensely interested in his story, and Defense Attorney Whiteman had to break this witness down in order to save his client. The grilling that Whiteman had given Sergeant Burnett seemed rather insignificant in comparison to the blistering attack that followed against Chapman.

Whiteman ranted and raved and accused Chapman of almost every crime in the book; he made him admit what an ingrate he was to turn on Mrs. VanDewater, who had befriended him in a number of ways, and he finally got Chapman to admit the reason for his turning on Mrs. VanDewater was the discovery of the unlicensed revolver by Sergeant Burnett. Whiteman then pointed out to the jury, in subtle questions to Chapman, the lengths to which the State Police and particularly Sergeant Burnett would go in obtaining evidence to support their charges. Subtly, he insinuated that this was a deal between Burnett, Chapman, and me, whereby Chapman would lie about the fire in order to escape punishment on the revolver charge.

The next morning, newspapers played up this feature of the defense, pointing out what a great miscarriage of justice this would be if such a charge were, in fact, true.

When it came to summation, Whiteman pulled out all the stops. He talked about everything from the Constitution and the Bill of Rights and the protections that these ancient documents represented and claimed these rights were being trampled upon. He rode the reputation of the State Police hard but then realized that Sergeant Burnett had a fine reputation locally, was an outstanding police officer, and that it had been a mistake to accuse him of the things that he had cross-examined him about. In a whining' trembling voice, Whiteman made a plea somewhat as follows:

"If I have said anything about my good friend Charlie Burnett, who in my opinion is one of the finest police officers in the State of New York, and who on many nights has employed his time protecting the people of this area and looking after our welfare in every possible way, and who has investigated these heinous crimes and done everything possible to keep the people secure in their thoughts that they were safe while criminals roamed the countryside, I want to apologize. I made such statements in the heat of battle. My emotions overcame me on behalf of my clients. I have the highest regard for Sergeant Burnett; I love him like a brother. But this other son of a gun, Chapman..."

He then went on to eviscerate Chapman, tearing him into legal pieces. One would have thought that it would have been impossible to hoodwink a jury on such an inconsistent hodgepodge, that they couldn't have been fooled in any way whatsoever.

In my summation, I tried to point out the inconsistent hodgepodge ladled out by the defense attorney. But there was a sense that the newspaper articles hammering away at the heavy punishment versus such a small amount of insurance, the subtle and almost libelous inferences about conduct in the case by the prosecution and the Court, and what was being called the unfairness of police authorities, all had their effect on the jury.

After a number of hours of deliberation, a verdict of not guilty was returned.

In the presence of the Court and the jury, Mrs. VanDewater turned to me and said, "Well, I did it just like Robley said, and you can't do a damn thing about it now that I have been found not guilty."

The jury had heard and stared in amazement at her and at me. Jaws dropped.

The verdict had been recorded, and there was nothing that could be done then. But we all knew the one thing that Mrs. VanDewater forgot: there was her suit against the Hartford Insurance Company to recover the amount of the insurance that had not yet been tried.

When this civil trial came up, and the facts were placed before the court, the jury found a verdict of no cause for action in favor of the Hartford Fire Insurance Company.

6

A GUILTY CONSCIENCE

Near the end of the primary campaign, on one of my visits to Canisteo, I dropped in on Joseph C. Latham, publisher of the *Canisteo Times*. Joe was an ardent Republican and afterward an aggressive Republican Committee County Chairman and someone who was helping me in my campaign.

During the course of our conversation about my campaign, he asked me if I knew Frank E. Storms, president of the Citizens National Bank at Hornell. I had to admit that I had never met Mr. Storms. Mr. Latham told me that he had seen Storms recently, that Storms was much interested in my campaign, and that he didn't care much for my brother-in-law, Guy W. Cheney, as a prosecutor. Latham suggested that I drop in at the bank and see him the first time I was in Hornell, which I promised to do. It being the closing days of the campaign, I did not get to see Mr. Storms.

As it later turned out, this was a very fortunate break for me.

During the VanDewater arson trial the following January, I went to the Seneca Lunch Room one noon with several of the Court attendants. We were followed in by County Judge Edwin S. Brown, who was presiding at the arson trial. Seated at the lunch counter were some friends of mine, Attorney Clyde Schults and Bill Hollands, who was president of the Steuben Trust Company. There were also several lawyers and a very distinguished-looking man whom I had never seen before. I shook hands with Clyde and Bill and the other lawyers and passed the time of day with them. Judge Brown came up also and did the same.

Then Judge Brown said to me, "Don't you know Frank Storms here?"

I said, "No, I have never met him," and then I shook hands with him and said, "Mr. Storms, I'm glad to meet you. I had been meaning to come to see you."

His face blanched, his hands started to tremble, and he had what appeared to be a heart attack right there at the lunch counter. One of the men gave him a drink of water. He took some kind of a pill and seemed to recover. Then, wonderingly, I moved on down to a table to get my lunch.

About an hour and a half after court had started that afternoon, one of the attendants approached and whispered to Judge Brown on the bench. The judge stopped court proceedings and said that I was wanted on the long distance phone, so they would take a five-minute recess.

On the phone was my friend, Joseph C. Latham, who said, "What did you want of Frank Storms this noon at the Seneca Lunch Room?"

"I just wanted to tell him," I said, "that I appreciated the nice things that you said he had spoken to you about me during my campaign, and I was sorry I was unable to get in to see him."

"Are you sure," Latham said. "Is that all?"

"That is all I had in mind," I replied.

"Latham asked, "Couldn't it have been something else?"

And I said, "Not a thing."

We then resumed the arson trial, and not over half an hour had elapsed when I was again called to the telephone. It was Latham again and he said, "I just talked with Frank Storms and he insists it must have been more than what you said it was."

I assured Latham it was not; that was all I had in mind, and I didn't know anything more I could talk to Storms about.

A few days after the trial had finished, Latham called me again at Corning and wanted to know if I wasn't holding something back about Storms. By that time, we had both become very curious, but between us, we were unable to resolve it.

In the meantime, Franklin D. Roosevelt was elected president at a time when serious economic conditions were enveloping the country, not the least of which was the failure of a number of banks. Immediately after his inauguration, he declared an almost unheard of, or at least unthought of, bank holiday, closing all the banks in the country for a few days and permitting them to reopen only after they had been preliminarily investigated and their opening was approved by government investigators. Hornell had three banks: Steuben Trust Company, the Citizens National Bank, and the First National Bank of Hornell. The First National Bank was unable to reopen.

Conditions got so bad in Hornell, and people became so alarmed that a run started on the other two banks. Many rumors were afloat in Hornell about the financial condition of each bank.

During this run on the banks, I received a call from Bill Hollands, president of the Steuben Trust Company, asking me to come to Hornell to see if the vicious rumors that were being circulated about the financial condition of each bank could in some way be stopped. Hastening to Hornell, 45 miles from my home in Corning, I called a meeting of the officers and directors of the two banks, which was held in the closed First National Bank of Hornell.

After discussing the matter with them and getting all the information they seemed to have, I advised them to make a joint statement about the sound financial condition of each bank. I further promised them I would immediately start a John Doe investigation in Hornell City Court and subpoena anybody who had been heard to express doubt about the soundness of the financial condition of the banks, try to find out where they got their information, and what the basis of the rumor was. We would get newspaper publicity about the investigation and warn people about criminal prosecution for spreading false rumors, and thus, with the threat of such prosecution against those who are dispensing such false rumors without actual knowledge, we might be able to head off the runs on the banks.

While I was attempting to draw up such a joint statement to be signed by the officers of each bank, I turned to get some information from Bill Hollands and found that he had gone out to the men's room. As I looked toward the men's room, he poked his head out of the door and nodded for me to come down and see him. So I strolled down there alone, and he told me, in strict privacy, "I am perfectly willing to issue a statement about the soundness of our bank and have all the officers sign it and publish it. I know our bank is sound. Our assets are liquid enough, and we can survive this run, but I don't know anything about the Citizens National Bank, and I will not sign or have any of my officers sign a joint statement vouching for the soundness of that bank."

I could see he was disturbed and troubled, and while he said that was all he knew, I sensed he had at least some suspicions about the soundness of the other bank. The most I was able to get from the officers, therefore, were individual statements about the soundness of each bank.

I promptly started the John Doe investigation with employees, and we managed to slow down the rumor-mongering and the runs on the bank. In the meantime, the Federal Government sent bank examiners to each bank. They discovered shortages in the Citizens National Bank and talked first with the bank's president, Frank E. Storms.

That night, after being questioned by bank examiners, Foster Woodbury, the bank's cashier and trust officer, abruptly committed suicide. The Federal Government promptly closed the bank and appointed Horace Mizzell as a temporary receiver of both the Citizens Trust Company and the First National Bank of Hornell.

Mizzell, as receiver, immediately took over those banks and went through their books, accounts, and records. He discovered in the Citizens National Bank a shortage of more than $100,000. Since it involved a national bank, this matter he laid before the Federal Grand Jury, which returned an indictment in U. S. District Court for the Western District of New York against Frank E. Storms and Samuel Norton, a teller of the bank, for embezzlement. Whether the cashier, Woodbury, was guilty of embezzlement or merely had guilty knowledge thereof and didn't choose to betray his friends was never publicly disclosed.

Storms and Norton were arrested and released on bail. A number of months went by until, in the latter part of August 1932, a prominent Hornell citizen asked me as D. A. to meet with some other prominent citizens. These men had previously formed an investment group they called "The Exchequer Club," an unincorporated association in which Frank E. Storms was the secretary and treasurer. Each member of the club had put in from $10 to $50 a month, and Storms, as treasurer, would invest the money in securities. And they were, if not concerned, at least worried.

Annually, the members would have a meeting in the directors' room of the Citizens National Bank. Storms would bring out the securities, which were supposed to belong to The Exchequer Club, and they were checked over by the members present. Storms would then be complimented upon the sound way in which he was investing the assets. Each member was furnished with a typewritten copy of his report listing the securities, and they then held a dinner at a well-known social club in celebration of the fine way in which the "Nest Egg" of The Exchequer Club was growing.

These members of the club advised me that at least some of the securities that were supposed to belong to the club were claimed by Federal Receiver Mizzell to belong to some trust funds of the bank. They were afraid matters were moving too slowly in the Federal Court. In fact, they had other fears and felt they would be left out in the cold, with the Federal Government having no jurisdiction over Storm's private actions in their club.

They knew very little about the workings of the Federal Court, about the way in which such matters were handled, or how slowly it sometimes took the Federal Government to bring such cases to trial. Some of them even went so far as to charge that they thought there was a "fix" somewhere along the line that would enable Storms to get out of this difficulty without punishment.

I assured them that this was not so, but they wanted me to investigate their club accounts thoroughly and if evidence was found that Storms had used some of the securities of The Exchequer Club for his own use, to seek an indictment against him.

I immediately took this up with the receiver of the bank. We investigated all of the accounts of The Exchequer Club and various trust accounts in the bank. We found that some of the securities that Storms had listed as being owned by The Exchequer Club had turned up in the safety deposit boxes of various bank trusts, and the receiver was claiming them for the bank trust accounts by virtue of the fact that they were listed as trust account assets and were found in trust account safety deposit boxes.

The Exchequer Club was more than $100,000 shy in assets that could be definitely claimed by the club. Through Storms' annual statements to members of the club, we were able to sort and trace at least $40,000 of those securities that had been in the various trust safety deposit boxes and listed as assets for the respective trusts. I, therefore, put this matter before the September Grand Jury, which indicted Mr. Storms for embezzlement of The Exchequer Club funds.

He was promptly taken into custody on a bench warrant and arraigned before Honorable Edwin S. Brown, Steuben County Judge, who was a great personal friend of Storms.

It was then that I realized why Storms had turned pale when I had been introduced to him by Judge Brown in the Seneca Lunch Room in Hornell and had told him that I was coming in to see him and why he had gotten our mutual friend, Joseph C. Latham, and a stockholder to the extent of $30,000 in his bank, to try and find out the reason. His sudden heart attack in the Seneca Lunch Room was certainly his guilty conscience erupting.

Upon arrest, Storms immediately called his attorney, John W. Hollis, one of the best-known and ablest trial attorneys in the area. John also was representing him in the indictment in the Federal Court. Although Storms was out on bail, he was to appear the following Monday in Federal Court in Canandaigua, New York, for either trial or change of plea.

On Friday, Attorney Hollis appeared on the arraignment of Storms in County Court before Judge Brown, who immediately said he would have to disqualify himself as Storms was too close a personal friend. Attorney Hollis told of the forthcoming appearance on Monday in Federal Court and demanded release without bail until the Federal case could be disposed of.

This I refused to consent to; substantial bail was required.

Hollis accused me of being a czar, of wanting everybody in jail, and of unjustly keeping them there. Hollis said he wouldn't allow his client to put up bail but would notify the Federal Court that I was holding him and trying to defeat the Federal Government in their prosecution. I told him to go ahead and do this.

Evidently, he called Federal Judge Knight in Buffalo, who phoned telling me he heard from Mr. Hollis that I was trying to throw a monkey wrench into the prosecution of Storms by the Federal Government, and that I should release Storms at once so that he could come to Canandaigua for trial or change of plea the following Monday. I told Judge Knight that I owed just as much of a duty and responsibility to the people of my County as to the Federal Government; that this man was accused of stealing $40,000 from The Exchequer Club and had probably taken many thousands of dollars more, which we so far hadn't been able to conclusively establish, so I didn't propose that he get away from me.

Judge Knight then wanted to know why I wouldn't release him without bail. I asked him whether he wanted it glossed over or straight from the shoulder, and he said to give it to him straight. So I told him that there was talk among some of the members of The Exchequer Club that the "fix" was on in Federal Court.

Judge Knight let out a an ear-splitting roar over the phone and said, "You send him over to me. I will take care of him."

After he had calmed down, I told Judge Knight Storms would probably pay the bail and be there on Monday, but if he didn't put up bail, he was going to stay in the Steuben County Jail.

The upshot of it was that Storms did put up a $50,000 bail bond and one of the men who signed his bond was Dr. Otto K. Stewart, one of the largest investors in The Exchequer Club that Storms had defrauded!

On Monday, in Federal Court in Canandaigua, Storms changed his plea from not guilty to guilty. Judge Knight promptly sentenced him, in spite of the pleas of his counsel that he had an involved heart condition, to 1½ to 3 years at the Federal Penitentiary at Lewisburg, Pennsylvania. Although the amount embezzled was more than $100,000, the judge was undoubtedly influenced by Storms' physical condition and also by the fact that a light sentence such as this to a man of Storms' sensitive upbringing and position in society was more punishment than a longer sentence would have been to a less sensitive and younger man. Storms at that time was about 60 years of age.

Norton also pleaded guilty and was sentenced to a year and a day in the same Federal Penitentiary at Lewisburg.

A few months after Storms had been in Lewisburg Penitentiary, his attorney, Mr. Hollis, came to see me and begged me to dismiss the county indictment against Storms. Hollis said that Storms had been examined not only by his own doctor but by the physician at the jail. Both agreed that Storms could never live out his term, even with time off for good behavior, if he had to serve it in jail. Hollis claimed, however, that Storms couldn't get a reduction or commutation of his Federal sentence until this Exchequer Club indictment in Steuben County was dismissed.

At the time, I thought this was one of Hollis' tricks and that he was exaggerating, so I refused to consider such a plea. Several weeks later, Hollis brought Storm's wife in to see me. She made a very tearful appeal for a dismissal of the indictment so he could at least attempt to be released from the Federal Penitentiary and thus give him a chance to live. I could see she was a fine woman, and there was no questioning her honesty or sincerity. Again, I felt I had to refuse, although I had a great deal of sympathy for Mrs. Storms. I had a responsibility that I couldn't dodge.

A few weeks afterward, Hollis asked me to appear before Judge Brown to discuss dismissal of the indictment. We had a rather angry and bitter session. I finally told Mr. Hollis that if I could arrange it with the Federal government, I would have Storms brought into Steuben County under Federal guard and try him on our indictment. That would settle it once and for all. Hollis had maintained that I could never convict Storms under the indictment we had against him.

Judge Brown became angry and said we wouldn't try Storms before him under any circumstances.

I reminded the judge that he had a long vacation coming, that he hadn't felt very well for a number of months, that it would be a good thing for him to take this vacation, and that we could call in some other judge from an adjoining county, and then he, Judge Brown, would not have to preside over a criminal trial of a personal friend.

Hollis finally wound up by denouncing me, saying, "I never want to see you again. You aren't even a human being," and that "if I do see you, I won't speak to you, and don't you speak to me."

Several weeks after that, Storms died in jail, just as Hollis had predicted.

Of course, I felt sorry, but I still thought that I had done the right thing because Storms had not only caused the failure of the bank with great monetary loss to its depositors, which was a federal matter, but he had stolen from his close personal friends, who had honored him and trusted him in every possible way. He also had betrayed his duties as secretary and treasurer of The Exchequer Club.

I have often wondered why Storms needed or wanted so much money in a small city like Hornell—$100,000 from the bank plus $100,000 from The Exchequer Club. No mention was ever made of what became of the embezzled funds. He didn't offer to make restitution, so he must have spent $200,000. On what?

It was some nine or ten months after that before John Hollis would speak to me again. This was unfortunate for he and I had been friends, and he had helped me in my primary campaign, but such is the life of a district attorney.

7
A HOUSE IS NOT A HOME

A few months prior to my taking office, the State Police had arrested a woman in the town of Corning by the name of Lola Carpenter for keeping a disorderly house, together with four or five other girls. They were all taken before the justice of the peace of the town, and none of them at that time had prior records or convictions. When they all pleaded guilty, the justice of the peace severely admonished them about such a violation of law but suspended their sentence on the condition that they leave the town of Corning immediately.

This they did, and the matter was soon forgotten. Several months after I had taken office, however, a deputy sheriff called me on the phone and said that a young woman up in Addison had gone to the public library and wanted to borrow books regularly. The librarian asked her where she was living and gave her a card to fill out on which she was required to give her name, place of residence, her occupation, and the answers to several other questions.

Under "occupation," she wrote the word "whore."

When the old maid librarian looked at that, she was flabbergasted, but she allowed the woman to take the book and then immediately called in the Addison Chief of Police, Elmer Bovee, who got in touch with the deputy sheriff, Lester C. Andrews, one of the two investigators assigned to assist me. I advised Andrews to get a warrant for this girl's arrest and also to get a search warrant. If there were any other girls at this residence (the chief of police seemed to know there were also four or five other girls there), he was to arrest them and charge them all with being inmates of a disorderly house.

This the chief and deputy sheriff did; the girls pleaded guilty without any hesitation. I appeared at their arraignment before the justice, and they readily admitted they had been running a disorderly house.

Not knowing anything about the prior case in the town of Corning and that these were the same girls, the justice of the peace, over my protest, suspended sentence on them. He placed them on probation and ordered them out of the town of Addison. This justice also thought they were nice-looking girls and that they wouldn't do it again.

A number of months later, the State Police found and reported that these same girls had gone back into a different part of Corning and set up in business again. The State Police, therefore, arranged to bring in a trooper who had never before been in this area, put him in plain clothes, and get him into the house. He was to pass some marked money for the sexual services to be rendered. Then, at a prearranged time, other police were to walk into the place and catch him in bed with one of the girls. This time, there would be no confessions involved, but we would have what appeared, at least, to be an actual occurrence with marked money.

The trooper brought in, of course, was a young bachelor who was eager to do everything he could to help the State Police in the enforcement of their work. The boys, however, thought they would play a trick on him. Instead of making the raid at the precise moment they had agreed on, they delayed about 15 minutes getting in there, and the young trooper was hard-pressed in his dealings with the girl who, unaware he was of "the law," had expected him to consummate everything that he had paid for.

The young trooper, however, was successful in stalling around until the uniformed troopers arrived.

All inmates, including the "madam" Lola Carpenter, were taken before a different justice of the peace. Under the advice of an attorney who was hastily called in, all pleaded not guilty. Bail was fixed, a date was set for trial, and a jury trial was demanded. In the meantime, the madam, Lola Carpenter, put up bail for herself but didn't furnish it for the girls. They were, therefore, incarcerated in the county jail pending trial.

At the jail, the girls were examined by the county physician. Blood tests and smears were taken. At the trial, the results of the blood test and smears were introduced into evidence. One girl had four plus syphilis, and three others were infected with gonorrhea. They were indeed "nice girls" to turn loose on an unsuspecting community.

At the time of the trial, the four girls changed their pleas to guilty and testified for the people. The only one tried was the madam, Lola Carpenter.

The jury promptly found her guilty, and the justice of the peace immediately sentenced her to serve the maximum—six months in the county jail—and to pay a fine. The other girls were given much lighter sentences with small fines due to the fact that they had turned State's evidence against the one who was primarily responsible for their predicament. None of these girls was over 25 years of age, and several of them didn't appear to be more than 18 or 19.

We found out later that these girls were part of a regular "white slave ring"; they had been shipped in from far and wide and would stay a few weeks or months at the outside and then would move on to some other unsuspecting village or city either here in New York State or in the adjoining state of Pennsylvania.

Corning bordered on the state of Pennsylvania, and girls from here would go many miles away to Erie, Pennsylvania, and from there perhaps to Wilkes Barre, Pennsylvania, or to Jamestown, New York, or elsewhere. They had a regular circuit where these girls were shunted and rotated from place to place.

The details about the circulation of women for immoral purposes or who was running this operation were never determined. We had strong suspicions but no legal proof; however, for the most part, we managed to keep them from Steuben County.

8

A CASE OF RAPE

Some months before I took office, a Hornell woman came home late one night looking a little bit worse for wear, and her husband accused her of being out with another man. She had been drinking, although not intoxicated, and she sobbed out to him that a man had forced her into his car and taken her for a ride and then raped her.

The husband immediately called the Hornell Police, and they, together with the Sheriff's Department, investigated the matter, and they then reported it to my predecessor.

On information, one Dennis Cadigan was arrested and charged with first-degree rape. The then D. A. put the matter before the next Grand Jury and sought an indictment against Cadigan. The whole evidence seemed to revolve around the question of the veracity of Cadigan or the woman.

Cadigan, on being questioned, admitted he had been out with the woman and said that she had willingly consented to have sexual intercourse, that she had voluntarily agreed to get into the car with him and go for a ride for that purpose.

The woman, of course, told an entirely different story. Her

clothes were disarrayed and slightly torn. These facts were put before the Grand Jury, but the Grand Jury found "no bill," and Cadigan was released.

The husband was outraged and incensed by this action as his wife had convinced him that she was telling the truth. He not only wrote to most of the judges in this Federal district, who had nothing whatsoever to do with the enforcement of state law in Steuben County, but finally wrote to the governor of the State of New York, The Honorable Herbert Lehman, demanding justice.

Just as I came into office, I received a communication from Governor Lehman directing me to resubmit the case to another Grand Jury. On familiarizing myself with the facts of the case and finding that Cadigan previously claimed that there had been no rape but that the Intercourse had been voluntary, I suggested to the Grand Jury that in view of the fact of the governor's interest and that the evidence came down to a question of who was being truthful, they could indict Cadigan for rape with a second count of adultery. Although the proof was a bit thin, they had enough corroboration of her story with her torn clothes. Also, Cadigan admitted that he had taken her in his car out into the country for the purpose of seducing her. This latter count he couldn't escape in view of his prior admissions.

That's exactly what the Grand Jury did.

The husband, at first, was rather incensed that I should even suggest such a possibility. But I calmed him down and assured him that our objective was not to take any chances on the trial jury's being fooled by Cadigan's slick attitude, as was the first Grand Jury, but to make sure that he got punishment of some kind.

To the surprise of everybody, when Cadigan was arraigned on this indictment, he appeared with an attorney, George A. King, and pleaded not guilty, not only to the rape but to the adultery, and repudiated any prior talks he had had with the officers as to his having sexual intercourse with this woman.

After a rather brief but vigorous trial, on March 3, 1932, the trial jury did exactly what I figured they would do, bringing in a verdict of guilty of adultery. I duly reported the outcome of this to Governor Lehman, and I'm sure that he and his counsel must have had a good laugh. The strange thing about the whole affair was that when it was all over and the man had been sentenced, the husband was perfectly satisfied and stood reunited with his wife. They then left the courthouse arm in arm together.

Attorney George A. King, who defended Cadigan, was a very able, aggressive, and resourceful trial lawyer who afterward became district attorney and later county judge of this county.

9
A SHOOTING

The early cases in the winter and early spring of 1932 were run-of-the-mill: forgery, abandonment, burglary, driving while intoxicated, illegal sale of liquor, and other minor crimes. In March of 1932, however, rather early one cold, bitter evening, I received a call from Corning City Police headquarters that a man had been shot and was dying in Corning City Hospital.

I immediately hurried from my home to police headquarters and from there to the scene of the shooting.

The chief of police had already stationed an officer at the hospital to talk with the man who had been shot when he regained consciousness. The victim turned out to be one Arthur Appleby, and I instructed the police to notify me as soon as he could talk. The "house" in which he had been shot was located on Watkins Avenue on the Corning-Watkins Glen Road, just where the city joined the town of Corning.

It seems that about 8:30 that evening, the police received a call from a man on Watkins Avenue near the northern city line informing them that Appleby had just stumbled into his home and collapsed. He was bleeding to death from a shot in the groin. An ambulance and a doctor were rushed there immediately; he was given first aid, and he was just able to give them some bare facts before he went into a coma.

He had been shot in a house about 200 yards north of where the police found him. Investigation showed there was a big pool of blood in the living room of the house, another one on the front porch, and several pools where he had dragged himself along the highway. The house where the shooting occurred was deserted, although the lights were on and the doors were open.

Appleby was a glass worker and in his spare time repaired automobiles. Someone had brought a Cadillac to him for minor repairs and a tune-up, and after Appleby had finished repairing the car, he decided to give it a road test. He dressed up in his best clothes and drove to Watkins Glen, which was 22 miles away, looking for a good time.

There, he had several drinks and then drove back on the main Corning-Watkins road to this place, which was occupied by two men, Anthony Garfield (whose real name was Antonio Garfino) and John Cannizzaro, both of whom came from down near South Waverly, Pennsylvania, just over the line from Waverly, New York. They were apparently well known in Waverly. Tony had relatives, as I remember, either his mother or an aunt who lived on Railroad Avenue in Elmira, New York.

Also in the house where the shooting occurred was a local character called Gus, who acted as a general handyman and dispenser of drinks. There were several girls who were apparently there both for immoral purposes and for rolling drunks.

When Appleby drove the borrowed Cadillac up to this place, the proprietors were not immediately visible. Having seen the big car and Appleby well-dressed, they speculated mistakenly that this was some rich playboy who would be an easy mark. So, for the time being, they stayed out of sight.

Appleby went in, bought a couple of drinks from Gus for himself and two girls, and settled down to enjoy himself. Soon, he had a girl on each knee with his arms around them. While they were thus engaged, Cannizzaro and Garfield appeared at the door of the living room.

Cannizzaro wore a mustard color, chinchilla-looking, long overcoat with a gray slouch hat pulled down over his forehead. Garfield was bareheaded and wore a short, dark navy blue reefer overcoat. Cannizzaro had a .32 automatic in his left hand, and Garfield had brass knuckles on one of his hands. One of them yelled at Appleby to "stick 'em up."

Appleby was a big, strong, powerful man who was used to rough-and-tumble fighting. Instead of submitting and "sticking 'em up" as ordered, he dumped both of the girls onto the floor and made a grab for Garfield. They wrestled and fought, and Garfield was getting the worst of it. Cannizzaro, all this time, was watching his opportunity to shoot Appleby, but in the fracas, he didn't dare shoot for fear of hitting Garfield.

The girls ran screaming from the room and disappeared, never to be seen again. Gus, the bartender, also flew out of there.

When Garfield and Appleby separated for an instant, Cannizzaro shot Appleby right through the upper thigh and through the femoral artery. Immediately after, Garfield, with his brass knuckles, hit Appleby on the jaw, and Appleby dropped to the floor. They then tried to get his wallet, but Appleby still had strength enough to thrash around and make things unpleasant for both of them, so they lit out of there.

Events were hazy to Appleby, who had passed out, and on coming to, he staggered onto the porch where he again lost consciousness and fell down, for how long we don't know. There was quite a pool of blood in each place, indicating the timings. Then he staggered out onto the highway and, from another pool of blood, we judged he lost consciousness again. These blood spots ended at this house, where he finally obtained help.

The Corning Police, in the meantime, found out the names of Cannizzaro and Garfield. They notified the State Police, the Sheriff's

Office, and the Elmira Police, 16 miles away, because they had learned from somebody that at least one of these fellows came from a small town in that direction, South Waverly, Pennsylvania. They furnished the various other neighboring authorities with more or less accurate descriptions of these two young men.

The Corning Police eventually picked up Gus, the handyman, but by that time, he had poured himself full of liquor. For all practical purposes, Gus was in a comatose condition and couldn't talk. We found out afterward that he did this on purpose so he wouldn't have to testify to anyone about anything.

Among the police authorities notified were the State Police barracks and the chief of the Village Police of Waverly. Acting together, Corporal Brown of the Waverly State Police and the Waverly chief of police, whose name I have forgotten, hastened to the foot of Waverly Hill on Route 17, which was the main highway coming from Corning through Elmira into Waverly, to intercept any car containing two or more men of their description.

While Corporal Brown and the Village police chief were watching for cars coming from Elmira, a car wheeled out of one of the Waverly streets and turned the corner onto Route 17 toward Elmira, going very rapidly. Both officers recognized the driver as a relative of one of these men.

The Waverly police chief recalled that there were also relatives in Elmira located on Railroad Avenue, so they rushed to call the Elmira Police and told them what they had just seen and that it was possible that they might be going up to this relative's house. Very possibly, Cannizzaro and Garfield were already there.

Detective Lynn Brunner, who took the call, and his partner were at Elmira Police headquarters. They jumped into a car just as one of the uniformed policemen appeared. They picked him up and sped up Railroad Avenue to the home of this relative.

There was no sign of life; the house was dark and looked deserted. The detectives sent the uniformed policeman around to the back of the house to guard the back door; they went to the front door, rapped, and finally pounded on the door. No sound was heard from within, but they kept on pounding until a dim light appeared in the hallway. A woman of apparent Italian descent appeared at the front door and cried, "What you want, what you want?"

They said, "Is Tony here?"

She said, "I no see Tony for a number of weeks."

They said, "We are police officers. We want to come in and talk with you."

After some little parlaying, she finally reluctantly admitted them. She continued to protest and insist that neither Tony nor the other man, whom the detectives described, were there. She hadn't seen them for some time, although she did know them.

In the dim light, however, one of the detectives saw lying on a chair a rakish, gray slouch hat and a mustard-colored overcoat corresponding to the description given them by the Corning Police.

When she saw his eyes fastened upon those articles, the woman's eyes unconsciously went up toward the top of the stairway.

Detective Brunner realized right away that these boys were upstairs. He had come away in such a hurry that he had forgotten his gun, but unarmed, he dashed up the stairs and, waiting in the darkness at the top of the stairs were the two young men. He promptly put them under arrest, and the officers took them to Elmira police headquarters, where they phoned the Corning Police to come and get them.

In the meantime, Chief Eckess of the Corning City Police and I had gone to Corning City Hospital waiting to talk to Appleby. He had come out of his coma and was giving us some of the facts, which I have related here and which corroborated what the officers had deduced from what they had seen and picked up in the neighborhood of the crime. Soon, the officers arrived from Elmira with the two prisoners.

Appleby was in the emergency room of the hospital under some sedation and having a blood transfusion. When confronted by the two men, he shouted, "They are the ones," pointing to Cannizzaro. "He is the one who shot me."

Both of them promptly denied any connection with the crime.

This might have been a very important thing had Appleby died, for at that time, we thought it was possible, and even the doctors believed he would die. On my insistence, they had so notified Appleby, and we took from him a dying declaration of the facts as he remembered them. But he was a strong, healthy, rugged, vigorous young man, and he recovered very rapidly once the initial shock of the loss of blood was over.

The April Grand Jury promptly indicted both Garfield and Cannizzaro for assault in the first degree, which is, among other things, assault with a loaded firearm with intent to kill a human being or to commit a felony upon the person or property of the one assaulted in violation of Section 240 of the Penal Law of the State of New York. On their arraignment in Corning City Court, they both pleaded not guilty and were represented by Attorney Thomas F. Rogers of Corning, a very skillful, wily, and astute criminal defense lawyer. Mr. Rogers, or Tom, as he was known to us, had more experience than any other lawyer in the Southern Tier of the New York State counties.

Our county judge, Hon. Edwin S. Brown, was taken ill and was not able to preside at the ensuing County Court Term in Corning in May of 1932. He obtained as a substitute the Hon. Walter N. Renwick, county judge of Allegheny County, which adjoins Steuben County to the west. Judge Renwick was an old-time prosecutor and an excellent judge. He had had long experience dealing with criminals, both as a prosecutor and as a judge on the bench, yet he was an eminently fair, sound, able, and experienced judge. We felt that we were extremely fortunate in having him to substitute for our own ailing Judge Brown.

As the trial was to be held in Corning, where the crime had been committed and would take place within less than two months of the shooting, there was considerable interest, not only in police circles but among the general public, because of the fact that Appleby had barely escaped with his life. At the trial, Garfield and Cannizzaro were both represented by Attorney Rogers, who had appeared for them at the preliminary hearing.

There is no need to recount all the details of that trial, which lasted nearly a week, but several events occurred that are worthy of notice. Although I had closely questioned Appleby about all the facts and details of the shooting, he had not once even mentioned to me that he knew Attorney Thomas F. Rogers by sight. When Rogers came to cross-examine Appleby, however, he was very sarcastic. He insinuated that Appleby wasn't all that he appeared to be, that Appleby had a hidden past that wouldn't stand inspection.

I had cautioned Appleby about Rogers' tactics and had warned him to hold his temper at all costs. For once a witness can be made to lose his temper, the battle is usually half won by the cross-examiner. But Appleby forgot this warning. He got mad. Appleby and Rogers started accusing each other of various things. Judge Renwick had difficulty in restraining both of them.

Finally, in answer to one of Rogers' insinuations that Appleby was not what he seemed to be, Appleby accused Rogers of having a personal grudge against him. Rogers, forgetting the cardinal rule that governs all cross-examinations, snapped at him, "What right have you to say anything like that?" When Appleby then started to explain, Rogers tried to shut him off.

But I jumped to Appleby's defense and said to the court, "Your honor, in view of the insinuations made by Mr. Rogers about Mr. Appleby, I think he should be allowed to explain to the jury just what he had in mind and to fully answer Mr. Rogers' question."

Over Rogers' strenuous objection, the court allowed Appleby to continue, and he told this story in substance: "One evening when I was feeling tired," he said, "I was walking on West Market Street past a store that was owned by a well-known family. A nice middle-aged woman, whom I had known casually, the daughter of the proprietor, stood in the doorway. She seemed rather sad and was weeping. I stopped to pass the time of day and asked what made her look so sad. She told me that she had a broken heart. After talking for a while, she invited me inside the store and took me into the back living quarters, where we sat down and had a few drinks together. Then she tearfully told me how she had fallen in love with a certain well-known prominent man of Corning; they had been very close to one another, and he was going to marry her."

At that time, I happened to glance at Rogers, and I noticed that the back of his neck was getting red.

"She said," continued Appleby "he was so nice and so sweet to me, that I thought that everything was going to be fine. But as time went by, we couldn't agree on a marriage date, and his love seemed to cool off. Then," testified Appleby, "she started to cry. She said, You wouldn't think that such a well-known, professional man who was known all over this part of the state would do anything like that to a lonely, innocent girl like me, but he broke off our engagement. And would you like to know who that rat was? Here is his photograph. And who do you think that man in the photograph was, Mr. Rogers? It *was* you!"

The courtroom was in a pandemonium, and Rogers flushed way up to the back of his ears. After recovering his poise, Rogers moved to have the testimony stricken and moved for a mistrial. Judge Renwick ruled, however, that he had asked the question, and he had gotten the answer whether he expected it or liked it.

Rogers and I were close personal friends, but afterward, he accused me of deliberately setting up this trap for him. I told him I not only didn't set it up, but I hadn't known that Appleby even knew him. Rogers then told me of a Federal dope case that he had defended and that somehow or other Appleby had become involved in it, either as a spy for the Federal authorities or in some other capacity. It seems that Rogers knew lots more about Appleby than I did, and in some respects, Appleby knew lots more about Rogers than I did, also.

In the trial, Rogers made a strong point of the improbability of identifying the two accused defendants in the dim lights of the living room where Appleby was shot. He pooh-poohed the idea of anyone being able to identify a man with a gray slouch hat pulled down over his forehead and wearing a long mustard-colored chinchilla coat.

At great length, Rogers cross-examined all witnesses who had testified about this hat and overcoat, as well as the identification of Cannizzaro in the hospital at the time they confronted Appleby when we thought he was dying. Rogers made much of Appleby's being so weak and under sedation at that time.

Rogers had brought into the courtroom a big bundle, which he had carefully placed under his counsel table. He was rather secretive about it. I was curious, and so were my police officers, but we didn't let Rogers know of our curiosity.

Rogers, of course, had attempted to point out the inefficiency of the police and intimated that there were other clues they had overlooked. That's standard defense tactics the country over. He also dragged other red herrings across the evidence trail.

When Detective Lynn Brunner was testifying and told about spotting the gray felt, slouch hat and the mustard-colored chinchilla coat at Garfield's relative's house, Rogers went after him. Brunner, when cross-examined, was positive he could identify that coat from any other similar coat. Rogers laughed at this and had one of the court attendants put it on and pull the hat down over his eyes. He then asked him if he still thought he could identify that coat from any similar coat. Brunner very quietly said, "Certainly, I can."

Rogers made Brunner repeat this several times; then, reaching down under his counsel table, he took this large package, which had been there all day, opened it, and disclosed two more, identical coats. The jurors and spectators all craned their necks with intense interest, sensing what was coming up. Rogers then got Brunner to say that he could still identify the coat that Cannizzaro had worn that night when he had arrested him and taken him to the Elmira Police Station.

Selecting three court attendants of about the same size as

Cannizzaro, Rogers had each one put on a coat and turn around before the court, before the witness Brunner, and before the jury. I am certain I couldn't have told one coat from the other, but I also felt certain that Brunner must have some positive reason why he stoutly maintained he could distinguish the coat that Cannizzaro had worn that evening from any other similar coat. Rogers made a big play of this demonstration; he taunted Brunner and ridiculed him about being able to identify such strikingly similar, mustard-colored chinchilla overcoats, but Brunner stuck to his story.

Rogers then had the court attendants take off the coats, and he carefully folded each one up, cleared off his large counsel table, laid the coats on the table, and shuffled them around like gamblers do in a three-card monte game. Grabbing one of the coats after he shuffled them for a while, he held it up above his head and yelled at Brunner, "Is this the coat that Cannizzaro wore?"

"Let me see the coat, Mr. Rogers," Detective Brunner said quietly.

"No, tell me," Rogers yelled. "I insist that you answer yes or no; is that the coat?"

I jumped to my feet, objecting that witness Brunner should be allowed to examine the coat.

The judge sustained me and ordered the coat to be passed up to Detective Brunner.

All this while, Rogers was smiling and smirking. Not only his clients but the jury and spectators were enjoying the whole scene. Some of the jurors even looked skeptical. Brunner, however, calmly and carefully looked the coat over. He looked in the sleeves and the lining, in the back under the collar, and very quietly handed it back to Mr Rogers, saying, "Yes, Mr. Rogers, that is the coat."

Rogers laughed and chortled and even snorted out his disbelief. Many of the spectators also left, and some jurors looked doubtful, some quizzical. Rogers again had the three attendants put the coats on and asked, "Do you see any difference in those coats?"

"Not from here, I don't," said Detective Brunner. "But you just let me take it, and I will tell you it's the one Cannizzaro wore."

"That is all," said Rogers, and he smiled triumphantly and sat down.

I was puzzled, for I had examined that coat many times; also, I had examined the other two coats while this demonstration was going on. I couldn't have told one coat from the other. I knew, however, that an experienced investigator like Brunner must have some sound reason for being so positive. So, very quietly, I said, "Mr. Brunner, will you please explain to the court and to the jury and to Mr. Rogers just why you are sure that this coat that I have in my hand is the one that Mr. Cannizzaro wore at the time of the arrest in Elmira."

"If you will look under the label and the lining you will find in small letters in indelible ink my initials and the date when I arrested him and had him in the Elmira Police Station," replied Detective Brunner.

That settled that issue and ended all questions of identification. The court had difficulty in restraining the laughter and nods of affirmation that went not only through the spectators but through the jury. A fine, careful, and well-trained cop's experience had paid off.

Rogers, however, had another ace up his sleeve. He had maintained all the time that his clients were not in Corning that night but in Elmira, participating in a card game of some kind down there. The officers had noticed that each day of the trial two or three young men, whom they had finally identified as being from Elmira and South Waverly, were present and appeared much interested in the trial.

Through underground sources that permeate every courtroom and every trial of this kind, we had picked up information that Rogers' ace in the hole was the standard defense of an alibi. We figured, therefore, that these men from Elmira and South Waverly or the vicinity were to be Rogers' alibi witnesses.

Sergeant Burnett said, "We can take care of them without any difficulty. A couple of my men have noticed them coming up through Gibson each morning this trial has been in progress. (Gibson is a small hamlet just east of Corning.) Undoubtedly, they will be in a hurry tomorrow morning, so I will station a couple of my men down there at the east end of Gibson to pick them up if they violate the speed limit."

That's exactly what happened. The following morning, these three men came wheeling through Gibson, which had a 30-mile speed limit, at some 45 or 50 miles an hour. The State Police promptly apprehended them and took them before a justice of the peace down there in spite of their protestations that they had to be witnesses at a trial in Corning. The State Police were leisurely and managed to stall things for about three hours, and it was nearly noon before Rogers' prospective alibi witnesses got loose from the justice of the peace.

When Court opened in Corning that morning, we noticed Rogers and the defendants looking around uneasily; they couldn't spot their friends in the audience. Rogers asked for a recess. He said that important witnesses had been subpoenaed and were due there. After more than an hour of waiting, Rogers finally decided that he wouldn't need the alibi witnesses after all, and we closed the case. When the witnesses finally did arrive, we were in the midst of summations, so they never got the chance to testify and perjure themselves.

Unfair? At first blush, one might say probably so, but my experience taught me to do everything that was possible to defeat phony evidence and stop witnesses from committing perjury. I never hesitated to do unto crooks legally what they would like to do to me illegally.

The jury, without any hesitation, brought in a verdict of guilty of assault in the second degree. Judge Renwick then promptly sentenced them to 2½ to 5 years in the State Prison at Auburn and fined each one $500 with one day additional for each dollar of the fine unpaid.

Garfield had been previously convicted of running a disorderly house in Bradford County, Pennsylvania, and on the same charge, which was a violation of Section 1146 of the Penal Law of the State of New York in the city of Elmira. Cannizzaro had one conviction for violation of the liquor law of the state of Pennsylvania in Bradford County. A couple of nice boys.

A number of years afterward, after I had become a judge of Surrogate Court, Steuben County, the same Anthony Garfield appeared in my chambers one day. I recognized him immediately. He seemed very friendly and showed no apparent animosity toward me for prosecuting him and sending him to State Prison. He told me that he had served his sentence, gotten time off for good behavior, paid his fine, and he learned his lesson. He said he was now trying to get established in the trucking business and needed a chauffeur's license, but before he could do so, he had to have a statement from either the prosecutor or the judge before whom the case was tried that they had no objection to his being granted such a license.

I questioned him rather closely, and he seemed sincere in this apparent effort at rehabilitation. I dictated a statement to my secretary that I had no objection for his use on such an application. While waiting for the statement to be typed, I asked him whether I had upset his plans in arresting his witnesses.

He allowed that he was rather glad of it; he was reluctant to involve them and was relieved they didn't have to commit perjury for him. He told me, in all frankness, that the case that we had built against him was just as Appleby said it had happened on the night of the shooting.

10

BROTHER VERSUS BROTHER

During the summer of 1932, nothing unusual from a prosecutor's standpoint took place except for a series of burglaries that occurred, mostly up and down State Highway Route 15, in the valleys of Bath, Kanona, Wallace, Cohocton, and Wayland. These burglaries were entries and thefts entirely from business places. They had the Sheriff's Office and the State Police worried. They were running around in circles trying to stop these burglaries.

Finally, through the combined efforts of the police, it was determined that three brothers, Edward Forrester, Alvin Forrester, and Kenneth Forrester, were the guilty ones who were committing these crimes. On the basis of evidence dug up by the police, we indicted them for the burglary of one of these business establishments.

Edward and Alvin were rough, tough, grown-up men. Kenneth, a younger brother under twenty years of age, was a weak character. The sheriff and the undersheriff talked to him when he was in jail awaiting trial and tried to convince him that he would do better pleading guilty. Kenneth, for some reason, while under arrest awaiting trial, had gotten into a disagreement with his brothers. He became so mad and disgusted with his brothers that he advised the sheriff he would plead guilty and testify for the prosecution.

The case was tried in Bath on July 20 and 21, 1932, before the same Judge Renwick, as Judge Brown was still laid up after his heart attack. The case itself was routine and not noteworthy except for the turning of one brother against two of his brothers. The jury found both of them guilty of burglary in the third degree, and the judge sentenced Edward and Alvin each to one to three years in Auburn State Prison. For turning State's evidence, Kenneth received only an indeterminate sentence to Elmira Reformatory, the execution of which was suspended during good behavior, and he was placed on probation. The sheriff's force and I all felt that young Forrester was the victim of domination by his older brothers. Now he would have a green light to make his way on the right side of the law. Suffice it to say, the burglaries up and down that valley ceased.

11
SERIOUS ASSAULT IN A ROADHOUSE

One of the two deputy sheriffs who had been assigned to make investigations for me was Howard Travis. Howard was a brilliant young man, about 5' 6", weighing over 200 pounds. He was commonly called "Tubby." He had two years in law school but had been unable to finish for financial reasons. On his appointment as a deputy sheriff, he had seriously taken up the study of criminology.

Deputy Sheriff Travis had heard through some of his underground "stoolie" connections that a man by the name of Charles LaPlaca had been driven out of Rochester, where he had been engaged in illicit liquor trade and some other nefarious transactions that violated or at least skirted, some of the provisions of the Penal Law. The stoolie reported that LaPlaca had sought more innocent and fertile grounds to operate here in Steuben County. He chose the town of Hornellsville, a few miles outside of the city of Hornell, on what is known as the Almond Road. Travis placed him under scrutiny for a few weeks but had not been able to get any evidence of a violation of the law.

Late one evening in October 1932, however, Travis received a "hurry-up" call that a man by the name of Guy Washburn had just been stabbed and had been taken to one of the Hornell hospitals. Travis raced to the hospital and found that Dr. Arthur Karl was treating this man, who had received a stab wound through the lung just below his heart. The doctor described the type of instrument that had been used as a long, thin-bladed knife or stiletto of some kind.

Travis learned from Washburn that the stabbing had occurred in LaPlaca's place and that LaPlaca had done the stabbing. Washburn further told Travis that LaPlaca was running a disorderly house up there and had a couple of girls for hire, as well as another woman with whom he was living. He said LaPlaca was selling liquor and that this woman, whose name was Blanche, called herself LaPlaca's common-law wife. She was renting upstairs rooms where customers would take the girls for immoral purposes. Washburn admitted he had gone there for the usual reasons. Travis promptly obtained a warrant against LaPlaca for assault second-degree, viz., an assault with a deadly weapon.

LaPlaca was arrested but was unable to furnish bail, waived examination, and was held for the Grand Jury. The November Grand Jury in Corning promptly indicted him for this assault, and he was tried in Corning before Hon. Edwin S. Brown, our Steuben County judge, who had recovered from his heart attack. The jury trial commenced on December 12, 1932. The attorney defending him was Niles Eddie from Rochester.

On arrival in Corning, Mr. Eddie had announced to some of the court attendants and police officers that he had come down from Rochester to show the "hicks" of rural Steuben County just how such a criminal case should be defended. He might better have stayed in Rochester because he wasn't anywhere near the equal of some of our better trial attorneys.

As the time for trial approached, it became obvious to us that, if possible, we must find the instrument with which Washburn had been stabbed. Without this instrument, we had just the doctor's testimony as to the extent and nature of the wound and the probable kind of knife or stiletto that had been used. We felt that if we could find that weapon, our case would be much stronger.

Right after the stabbing, on a search warrant duly obtained from a local justice of the peace, we searched the roadhouse and talked with Blanche and her girls. There, we found what the officers assured me were all the necessary accoutrements of a well-run disorderly house. So we had Blanche and her girls arrested.

We charged Blanche with being the "madam" and the girls with being inmates of a disorderly house. But there was no evidence found in the house of a knife or any other weapon fitting the doctor's description. Finally, a few weeks before the trial, Deputy Sheriff Travis received a tip through one of his "stoolie" connections that a knife had been hurriedly wrapped in a towel along with two loaded revolvers and buried in a rabbit hole several hundred yards back of the house toward the river bank.

Travis and several other deputies immediately scoured that area until finally, as they were about to give up searching, one of them stepped into a rabbit hole that had been recently and hastily covered over with grass and twigs.

On reaching down into the hole, sure enough, there was a dirty towel which, when unwrapped, contained two revolvers: one a large caliber pearl-handled pistol and one small caliber, plus our long-sought knife. We rushed the knife to the county laboratory, where the county pathologist, Dr. Rudolph J. Shafer, an expert in his field, found traces of human blood on the knife blade and furthermore determined that this blood was of the same type as Washburn's blood.

Up to the time of the trial, I had never personally made any examination of the revolvers, but I told Deputy Sheriff Travis to rewrap them in the towel just as they had been when found in the rabbit hole. This rabbit hole, by the way, was on the land occupied by LaPlaca's house. When Travis was testifying on the stand and was telling of the search that had been made and the finding of these two guns and the knife, in order to dramatize the production of those weapons, I took hold of one end of the towel and whipped it to let the guns and knife fall onto the table.

One of the guns fell onto the floor, and Deputy Sheriff Travis yelled, "Look out, George, one of those guns is loaded!" I had forgotten to tell him to unload the guns before he brought them into the courtroom. Travis thought they had to be, as evidence, in the same shape and condition in which they were found. That's the usual rule in a criminal case, from which loaded guns, bottles of poison, etc. are the exceptions. Judge Brown jumped right out of his chair and yelled, "Unload that gun at once."

Deputy Sheriff Travis and I both immediately apologized to the judge, and I unloaded the gun and went on with the trial. Dr. Karl then identified the knife exactly as he had described it even before he had seen it. He testified that, in his opinion, this would fit all the dimensions of the wound and could have been the knife that inflicted the injury. Fortunately, Washburn had recovered rapidly from the stabbing. The rest of the trial was routine, and the jury brought in a verdict of assault in the second degree.

Further investigation revealed that LaPlaca had prior convictions of grand larceny, first degree, for which he had served one year in the Monroe County Penitentiary, and corrupting the morals of an infant, for which he was sentenced to 2 ½ to 5 years in Auburn State Prison. In addition, he had served time for criminally receiving stolen property, for which he was sentenced to 10 years in Auburn State Prison, and had also been given a suspended sentence on a charge of petty larceny and of forgery.

We thereupon charged him as a fourth offender under the so-called Baumes Law. Judge Brown sentenced him to 25 years to life in Auburn State Prison—15 years to life for being a fourth offender and an additional 10 years for being armed with a dangerous weapon while committing a crime. At that time, LaPlaca was 28 years of age.

When Blanche, the so-called common-law wife of LaPlaca, heard the sentence, she screamed and fainted and flopped on the floor in the courtroom. Otherwise, this trial was uneventful, and Attorney H. Niles Eddie went back to Rochester with a new respect for small-town lawyers...hicks.

Some years later, I heard that LaPlaca, after serving his time in Auburn, was arrested, tried, and convicted of murder in Monroe County. Whether it was first or second-degree murder, I have forgotten. Unfortunately for society, such fellows seldom learn, and prisons are just institutions of detention, not reform.

12

THE BITCH

One fine early August day in 1932, two young fellows by the name of Orrin Wilson and Raymond Coon, ages about seventeen and eighteen years old, appeared at my office to tell me a weird story. They said there was an old fellow of the "Hillbilly type" by the name of David Hitchcock who lived in a shack up Meads Creek Road in the town of Campbell; and that Hitchcock had a grudge against one of the justices of the peace of the town of Campbell named John Fenton. This grudge arose out of some disturbance, as a result of which Justice Fenton had fined Hitchcock $5 for disorderly conduct. To Hitchcock, $5 would be as much as $500 to some other person.

They said that Hitchcock was bound to get even with Justice Fenton, and he had proposed to them that they burn Fenton's barn in revenge for the $5 fine. The boys appeared scared to death. On questioning, they said that they had become acquainted with him and had worked a little with him for some farmer. They said Hitchcock was of an ugly, vicious nature and, while not intelligent, was sly, cunning, and shrewd.

I asked them how Hitchcock proposed to burn this barn. They

said he had a little contrivance which he called the "bitch." It was merely the top of a baking powder can, which he would fill with lard. He would then take a narrow piece of cloth about 15" long, saturate that with lard, tie a small washer or even a stone near one end of it, and bury it in the lard in the top of the can, leaving the small end sticking out, like a candle wick. He would leave the long end trailing over the side of the can top. When lit, the result was just like a candle burning. The short end only would burn about an hour until all the lard in the top of the can was exhausted, and then the fire would travel down the wick over the weight and out along the longer part of the greased rag.

The boys said Hitchcock proposed to put this fiendish contraption in the hayloft of Fenton's barn. To make sure that the light of the burning wick could not be seen through a barn window from the house or the highway, he had a small box in which he cut air holes in each end. He proposed to put it over the contraption once it was lit.

The boys told me that they had asked him what he planned to do in case somebody discovered him. Thereupon, he pulled from one of his boots a long butcher knife that was ground down so fine and sharp that it could almost be used for shaving. Then he took from a drawer in a table two other smaller butcher knives similarly ground and sharpened, and he insisted that each boy take a knife. He would take the larger one, and if anybody interfered, they could defend themselves.

As the boys told me this story, their voices quavered, their hands shook, and they wanted to know what to do. They were thoroughly frightened. They said that he had demonstrated this "bitch" by lighting it and putting the box over it. It had taken about an hour for the lard to burn out and for the flames to eventually run down the rag and out onto inflammable material.

Davey, as they called Hitchcock, had told them that if necessary, in an hour's time, they could be in Pennsylvania or some other equally distant place and that no one would ever suspect their part in it.

I immediately got in touch with the sheriff's office, and we notified Fenton by phone of the situation. We would be up there after dark on the night of August 12th when this attempt was to be made. Sheriff Hoagland and Undersheriff Burleson came to my office to discuss the plan. We told the boys to go through with it just as Hitchcock had set it up. They said that his plan was to be at the barn about midnight.

That night, Sheriff Hoagland, Undersheriff Burleson, four deputy sheriffs, and I proceeded to a point about a quarter of a mile from Fenton's and then, in the darkness, walked up to the old farm. We didn't want Hitchcock to discover any extra cars around the place. We stationed several deputies outside the barn. This was a good gambrel-roof barn about 100 feet away from Fenton's house where he and his wife lived.

Barns under such circumstances in New York State are "within the curtilage," which means close enough to a house where someone is living as to endanger them in case of such a fire. The penalty for burning such a barn is the same in this state as burning an inhabited house.

The sheriff, the undersheriff and I then went inside the barn with two deputies. The three other deputies had stationed themselves outside at strategic places. Fortunately for us, the small barn door had a slightly squeaky hinge, so we deliberately left that door unlocked.

There were no domestic animals in the barn, but there was a loft full of hay and a ladder that led up to the loft. The ladder faced this small door. In the stillness of the night inside of the barn, we all squatted down in the mangers and stalls. The officers had drawn guns, both within and without the barn, and there we waited.

After about an hour, we heard the door squeak and thought it was Hitchcock. However, contrary to his orders, it was only an impatient officer who whispered, "Have they come yet?" and we whispered back, "No, get back to your post."

In the meantime, big barn rats were playing around on the barn floor, and I hate rats, especially large ones. About twenty minutes later, we heard the door squeak again, and this time we knew it must be Hitchcock. The plan was for Hitchcock alone to come inside the barn and leave the two boys outside to guard the place and sound the alarm in case of discovery.

The foolish deputy sheriffs stationed outside, when they realized the boys were present, and contrary to orders, grabbed the boys, and almost ruined the set-up. But after the door had ceased squeaking, I heard the ladder moving against the loose hay, and as these barn rats scurried around, the movement stopped.

Just at that time, one of these great big barn rats jumped on top of my head and stayed right there. Much as I hated rats and although quivering with excitement, I managed to keep quiet. The rat jumped again. Hitchcock must have sensed that this was a rat, and we heard the ladder jiggle again. Finally, everything was quiet.

Our plan had been to allow Hitchcock to light the "bitch," put the box over it, and catch him as he came down the ladder. The undersheriff, however, became impatient and itchy in the darkness and shined his flashlight up into the barn loft. There was Hitchcock in the loft, with the "bitch" in one hand and a match in the other. He was just about to strike the match on the box.

Sheriff Hoagland hollered, "Stop! I am the sheriff. I have officers both inside and surrounding the barn. They have guns trained on you. Come down without striking that match or they will shoot you."

Hitchcock hesitated for a moment, but he did come down the ladder and was immediately placed under arrest. Fortunately, no shots were fired and no matches were lit in a barn that was filled with dry hay.

I promptly had Hitchcock indicted by the next Grand Jury for attempted arson in the second degree. This was the willful attempt to burn or set on fire in the nighttime, a building not inhabited but adjoining or within curtilage of an inhabited building in which there was at the time a human being, so that the inhabited building was endangered even though it was not in fact injured by the burning, the attempt being a violation of Section 261 of the Penal Law covering such attempts to commit a crime.

We confidently expected under all these circumstances he would plead guilty. To our surprise, on arraignment, Hitchcock pleaded not guilty. He said that he had no money and demanded the assignment of counsel to defend him. Judge Brown assigned Hugh A. Varn, a young attorney from Addison, New York, who afterward became a very fine trial lawyer.

We had figured that once Varn became acquainted with the facts, he would bargain for a plea on a lesser offense or at least for a very moderate sentence. But Varn was young and ambitious and wanted trial experience, so we went to trial in Corning before County Judge Brown and a jury in the middle of October.

Varn's defense was a novel one. It was three pronged. First, the boys were to blame; second, Hitchcock was unlawfully entrapped into it; and third, as his principal defense he claimed there had been no overt act, and therefore, we couldn't convict Hitchcock of the attempted crime set forth in the indictment.

Surprisingly, Varn gave us quite a battle. First, on cross-examination he went after the two boys, Wilson and Coon. But they stood up nobly under Varn's attack and insinuations. Their promptness in coming to me in the first instance had stopped what could easily have been a very tragic occurrence. Then Varn went after me and the officers, claiming unlawful entrapment of his client. When that fizzled out, he put in what he thought was his real defense, lack of any overt act.

But catching the man in the hayloft with the "bitch" in his hand and a match ready to scratch and light it, and with a box to cover up the flame, plus being in another man's barn at midnight while armed with a razor-sharp butcher knife in his boot was too much of a handicap to overcome.

Judge Brown had left to the jury the question of whether stealthily entering the barn under such circumstances, climbing a ladder into a hayloft with those materials, and being caught in such a position didn't constitute such an overt act and an attempt to commit arson. The jury promptly convicted Hitchcock.

Before sentencing Hitchcock, the judge had him examined by some doctors as to his mental capacity. They found he had a mentality of less than a 12-year-old child. The judge, therefore, sentenced him to the New York State Reformatory at Napanoch, an institution for the criminally feeble-minded, on an indeterminate sentence. I understand he was never released from there.

It came out during the trial and was testified by both boys that Hitchcock had claimed to have successfully burned other barns in the same manner down in rural areas in Pennsylvania and had never been apprehended.

13
THE UNWRITTEN LAW

On Armistice Day, November 11, 1932, my wife and I went to Campbell, a little village nine miles northwest of Corning. There, I was scheduled to give a patriotic talk at the Presbyterian Church at a dinner celebrating Armistice Day. When we arrived and entered the dining room of the church, the pastor, Rev. George Parry, said there was a long-distance telephone call for me. He asked if I would have dinner first or take the call now. The phone being in the manse next door, I told him I had better take the call before dinner.

Mr. Abb W. Eckess, chief of the Corning City Police, was on the phone. He told me there had been a homicide. One Harry Wynes had shot and killed Loren Easton in the neighboring village of Riverside. He asked if I could come at once. I told him I would and cautioned him not to permit anybody to enter or touch anything until I got there.

I hurried back to the church, made my apologies, and told them I would be back in time to give the speech. As it turned out, I didn't finish investigating the case until 4:30 in the morning. Back at the church, after they had sung songs and hymns for more than an hour while waiting for my return, my wife volunteered to give the patriotic talk for me. The good folks present reported later that she made quite a speech. One of the Presbyterians was kind enough to bring my wife back home.

Arriving in Riverside, I went immediately to the murder house. When I got there, the police were busy interviewing people of the neighborhood and keeping the crowd away. I didn't want any precious clues destroyed. The hardest thing was to keep newspapermen out of the house. The eager news hawks were insisting on getting in there and taking pictures even before we had a chance to get the case buttoned up.

I found Chief Eckess seated in the prowl car with Harry Wynes. Eckess quietly and quickly told me the whole story. When he had gotten Wynes alone in the car, he realized that Wynes was near the breaking point. Eckess took a few minutes to calm Wynes down and then said, "Your friend Loren Easton (the murder victim) double-crossed you, didn't he?"

That set Wynes off, and he unfolded the whole sordid tale without reservation. After he finished his explanation, Chief Eckess sent Wynes temporarily to the Corning City Jail in the care of an officer. At my direction, he also sent Mrs. Wynes to the police station for later questioning. Then, the chief and I went into the house where the murder had been committed.

One of the bloodiest messes I have ever seen greeted me. Easton lay dead on the floor, shot to pieces in the stomach from a shotgun wound. Blood and guts were all over the place. We immediately got a local photographer who, before the body was moved, took pictures of everything at the scene.

The chief told me that both Wynes and his wife appeared intoxicated when he first arrived, but they seemed fairly sobered up then. Some hours later, both were considerably rational when I took statements from them in my office. They each talked freely and voluntarily in the presence of the chief, the sheriff, Trooper Lazeroff of the State Police, and some seven or eight of their other officers.

When we had finished with the photographer and our inspection of the scene of the murder, we went to my office to take statements from Wynes and his wife.

In the hall outside my office and in my waiting room a crowd collected, including newsmen, curious sensation seekers, and several lawyers. One of these, Thomas F. Rogers, probably the most successful criminal lawyer in the area, later became chief defense counsel.

On being advised of his right to counsel at all times, that he did not have to make a statement, and that if he did, it could be used in evidence against him, Wynes said he didn't want counsel. He wanted to get it over with and tell the *whole* story. This he did in the presence of all the officers and an official stenographer.

It was the age-old, sordid story of one man attempting to steal another man's wife. Wynes was a moody individual who'd had some brushes with the law before. With good reason, he had suspected that this man, Loren Easton, was ingratiating himself into his wife's favor. He had finally suspected and accused them of having intimate relations, which both denied. Wynes brooded about this for several weeks, during which time he and his wife quarreled bitterly.

On the day of the murder, Wynes had brooded to such an extent he started drinking early in the morning. Finally, in the afternoon, he and his wife and the man whom he had accused of being her lover got into an automobile together and drove around, stopping at various bars and having drinks. One such place we found was in Watkins Glen, some 22 miles away. Somewhere along the route, they had purchased a quart of liquor and some beer, which they took back to the Wynes' home. They arrived there in the early evening, and more drinking and quarreling followed.

Wynes told us he had planned the whole thing and that morning had carefully placed a loaded shotgun. Finally, he yelled at Easton, "I am going to end this thing once and for all."

Easton was almost too drunk to reply, but evidently realizing his danger, he grabbed a liquor bottle and threw it at Wynes, who ducked and fired both barrels at close range, hitting Easton in the chest and stomach, smearing and splattering his insides all over the room.

Wynes told us he had thought of killing Easton for several weeks but couldn't get up the nerve. That was why he drank so much liquor; he needed that artificial courage.

The Grand Jury indicted him two weeks later for murder, second degree, and I brought him to trial before Judge Brow and a jury in Bath on January 5, 1933.

Wynes had four defense counsel: Thomas F. Rogers as chief counsel, assisted by my brother-in-law, former District Attorney Guy W. Cheney, and his two law partners, Michael H. Cahill, who succeeded me as district attorney in 1936, and W. Earle Costello.

The legal defense was that of self-defense. Contrary to the statement she had given us the night of the murder, Mrs. Wynes repudiated her statement as having been induced by fear.

She testified that Easton had forced his attention on her and had threatened both her and her husband on a number of occasions. She further testified that on the night of the shooting, after they returned from the automobile trip, all were considerably under the influence of liquor. Wynes and Easton had quarreled over her. Easton started the quarrel and threw a liquor bottle at her husband and was in the act of picking up another bottle when her husband grabbed the shotgun to defend himself, and it went off by accident.

Of course, that was a phony defense because both barrels of the shotgun were discharged, and Mrs. Wynes hadn't mentioned or even intimated any such actions in the statement she gave me the night of the shooting.

The main defense, which in New York State is no defense at all and is illegal, was the so-called "Unwritten Law." Mrs. Wynes was obviously a very poor wife. She had sought the company of Easton, who already had a wife and two children. She had constantly quarreled with Wynes about this and other matters. She drank to excess and was a poor housekeeper. By these and other standards, she was a thoroughly undesirable woman. But her lover was dead, and she had no one to turn to except her husband. Her counsel, therefore, held her up to the jury as a paragon of virtue.

On the witness stand, she changed the story had initially given and now claimed that Easton had wormed his way into their family life, had forced himself on her, and that her husband had become insanely jealous, although she didn't want Easton's attention. She said they were trying to get rid of him, and that's what the row was about that culminated in the shooting. She claimed she was a poor, defenseless woman whom Easton had been taking advantage of in the absence of attention from her husband and that her husband resented these attempts to steal her affection.

The trial was the usual one in such cases. Under ordinary circumstances, it is almost impossible to prove to a jury's satisfaction that a woman is bad, so highly does the average man, in public at least, like to look upon womanhood. And to cap the climax, I freely admit that I fumbled the ball because of my inexperience in a case of this kind. I swore eight police officers as witnesses. One would have been ample. Eight made the defendant an instant underdog.

It's always a sound, standard defense tactic to attack police officers. In this case, the defense attorneys made a field day of it and attacked them all. Wynes repudiated his confession and claimed that he had been scared into it by so much show of authority. Each one of the officers was present when the confession was taken, and as sometimes happens, each one of them differed on some of the minor matters set forth in the confession. One officer, whom I shall not name as he is a close friend of mine, got all fogged up and disagreed with all the other officers on some of the major matters contained in the confession. There went the ball game. This, if nothing else, was enough to raise a reasonable doubt for any juror looking for an excuse to justify any decision based on the unwritten law that forbids in the minds of many men, toying with the affections of another man's wife. The jury retired at 3:42 in the afternoon and reached a verdict 12 ½ hours later at 4:20 in the morning.

Wynes had been told by his counsel that he had been tipped off by a court attendant who was in charge of the jury that he had been found guilty and that he should brace himself and not make any show at all. When the jury entered the courtroom, the clerk asked Wynes to rise and face the jury. He asked the foreman, "Have you agreed on a verdict?" The foreman responded, "We have. The defendant is not guilty!" It was too much for Wynes; he fainted and fell flat on his face in the courtroom.

Jurors afterward told me that in their minds, the unwritten law was the real defense even though they knew it was not legal and that the self-defense argument, together with the disagreement of the officers present at the confession, especially the one officer who disagreed with everybody about the important matters in Wynes' confession, constituted a sufficient excuse to raise a reasonable doubt in the minds of each juror about Wynes' guilt. This juror also said the jury wondered why more effort hadn't been made to blacken Mrs. Wynes' character, not realizing that a prosecutor is helpless in such matters on account of the strict rules of evidence. They had concluded, because of the lack of such proof, that she was entitled to the benefit of the doubt as to her character and chastity. For these reasons, the jury found Wynes not guilty because he was defending his name and her sacred honor.

Out of such mistakes, injustice sometimes triumphs.

During the course of the investigation, we found out that Wynes' wife, Grace, had possibly committed bigamy. The Grand Jury indicted her for that crime, but at trial was found not guilty. The shooting of Easton and the resulting acquittal of her husband was too fresh in people's minds, and the proof of bigamy was rather sketchy and inconclusive. Thereafter, we determined that during the bigamy trial, she had committed perjury, and the Grand Jury promptly indicted her for that crime, to which she pleaded guilty on March 29, 1933.

A few months after that, her husband, Harry Wynes, was arrested one evening by the local police for being intoxicated. As was usual with drunks, the officer placed him in one of the cells in the city jail adjoining police headquarters so he could sober up. The next morning, when the officer went to take him his breakfast, he found Wynes had hung himself in the cell. So ended the unhappy career of Harry Wynes and his unhappy relationship with Grace.

Thus, like water, hidden evil misconduct has mysterious ways of seeking and finding its ultimate level.

14

RING OF FIRE
(DEFRAUDING INSURANCE COMPANIES THROUGH ARSON)

For two years before I became district attorney, which, as I have pointed out, was during the last days of Prohibition, the police and fire departments of Hornell were greatly disturbed by a series of 35 incendiary fires. It seemed more than coincidence that each of those fires was at a place where police had suspected illegal liquor was being sold. Several of these places had been raided by the Federal government, as a result of which the proprietors had been found or pleaded guilty to violation of the Volstead Act. All of the 35 places and their contents were heavily insured.

Each of the fires took place under circumstances that aroused in the firemen and the police strong suspicions that they were of incendiary origin. Because of the heavy insurance, it seemed that all of the fires had been set for the purpose of "selling" their waning liquor businesses to the insurance companies. A representative of the arson department of the National Board of Fire Underwriters had investigated all of these fires. Both he and the police were morally certain (though without legal proof) that each fire was a "torch" job.

Although there was never enough evidence to justify arrests and criminal prosecution, in most cases, the insurance companies delayed payment of the claims while several civil suits brought by the insureds were pending. The companies defended their refusal to make payments by counterclaiming arson, but they were unsuccessful. Judgments were for the plaintiffs.

About 10:00 one evening, a few months after I had taken office in 1932, a fire alarm in the town of Hornell sounded for a fire at the home and restaurant of Joseph Arcieri on Loder Street, which was only three or four blocks from the Hornell fire station. The fire department, under Assistant Fire Chief Francis Kinnerney, rushed to the scene.

On arrival, they found the rear of the building a mass of flames. The firemen tried to put the fire out. As fast as they extinguished the fire on one wall, flames would jump and burst out on the opposite wall; when water was sprayed on the walls generally, the fire jumped all around.

As Assistant Chief Kinnerney was directing the fire fighting from the rear of the building, he noticed the fire chief, Platt Bond, who had just arrived, coming across the street toward the front of the building. He yelled at Bond, "The fire is in the rear here, Chief, come back here."

Chief Bond started running from the front of the building when Bang! There was a tremendous explosion that blew the whole front of the building across the street, just missing the chief as he ran from the front to the side of the building. It was quickly evident there was no possibility of saving anything except the surrounding buildings. And, there was no question but that this was an incendiary fire.

A strong petroleum smell permeated the atmosphere; the flames were dirty with black, oily smoke, and the flames bounced from wall to wall and back again as water and chemicals were directed at them. The Hornell Police, who were supervising the handling of the crowd that had collected, notified Police Chief Clarence Bailey and Deputy Sheriff Travis of the fire. Travis was one of the two investigators attached to my staff.

Travis and Bailey hastened to the scene, and as soon as things were cool enough so that they could get inside, they were able to salvage the remnants of the furniture, fixtures, and clothes. All of these had traces of oily substances and had a strong smell of petroleum. Deputy Sheriff Travis then phoned me in Corning. I told him to collect all of this material and pack what he could into airtight metal containers.

The following morning, I instructed him to take the evidence he had carefully collected to Dr. Paul Saunders, a professor of chemistry at Alfred University, 12 miles away, for analysis. In the meantime, he should have Chief Bailey keep the place under guard until it completely cooled down, and we could thoroughly examine the premises.

Dr. Saunders was a top-notch chemist. He not only taught the subject but specialized in industrial chemistry. Prior to this investigation, Deputy Sheriff Travis had talked with Dr. Saunders about the possibility of making some analyses of substances if the occasion arose. Travis called Dr. Saunders at once. Dr. Saunders told him to get the waste materials into large metal containers that could be sealed.

Following these instructions, the next morning, Travis took the materials to Dr. Saunders, who chemically analyzed and tested the bits of salvaged furniture and clothing. He found that they had been saturated with some sort of petroleum mixture, the exact chemical composition of which he gave to us. It had some scientific name which I do not remember. Also, Dr. Saunders reported that some of the greasy substance that had been scraped off the walls contained lard.

After making these tests, Dr. Saunders replaced the burned and saturated materials in these cans, sealed them airtight, and carefully marked them for use as evidence.

Grover C. Darrow, the representative of the Arson Department of the National Board of Fire Underwriters, was summoned from

Rochester. The next day, he, Chief Bailey, Travis, and I went searching and digging around in the cellar of the burned building.

The whole building was gutted, the roof was burned completely off, and there wasn't much left to examine so far as the walls were concerned. In the cellar, among the debris, charred ruins, and ashes, we found burned and destroyed old metal bedsteads, bedsprings, parts of a radio, a stove, an electric iron, and many other unidentifiable objects. But they were in such a burned and charred condition that it was impossible to tell their age or condition of newness before the fire.

All of the neighborhood people and friends of the Arcieri family were carefully questioned. We found that several days before the fire, they had gone on a trip to Pennsylvania. They were notified and immediately came home to find this mess. Joe Arcieri was a highly excitable man, and while we were questioning him, he became extremely agitated. He denied having anything to do with the fire and blamed it on some imaginary enemies whose names he did not know. He said he felt sure; however, it couldn't be anybody else.

In the meantime, he put in proofs of loss to several insurance companies listing a great deal of fine furniture, furnishings, tapestries, clothing, silverware, glassware, bric-a-brac, wedding presents, and other things worth many thousands of dollars. In the sworn proofs of loss to the insurance companies, he listed many articles of wedding gifts, all new, which he claimed had been given to one of the members of his family and had been stored there in the house. The insurance companies, of course, demurred at paying this loss. While they were still stalling, Arcieri brought suit in the Supreme Court against them.

Not until a year later did we get a break. A shady character, known by the Hornell Police and by Deputy Sheriff Travis to be skirting the fringes of the law, approached Travis one day and wanted a favor of some kind. When Travis asked him what he had to trade to get this favor, he said, "Would you like to know where the furniture and furnishings from Joe Arcieri's burned restaurant are stored?"

Travis immediately made a deal with the man, and he revealed, "If you search the place that Joe owns and has rented to someone up on the Almond Road about two miles outside of the city and is being used as a speakeasy, you will find what you are looking for."

Travis immediately phoned me in Corning, and I hurried to Hornell, 42 miles away. On the basis of this information, we secured a search warrant from a justice of the peace of the town of Hornellsville, and Travis and I and several other officers went up there.

The place was nice-looking and inconspicuously set back several hundred feet from the highway. It had a moderate-sized parking lot, a basement floor that went back into the sloping hill, a first floor that proved to be a dining and dance place, and a second floor that served as living quarters.

Entering at the basement level, we noticed a bar with tables set up in the usual speakeasy way. The place had a very small stock of liquor, which the proprietor had hurriedly but unsuccessfully tried to get under cover. We assured him we were not looking for that. There was no possible place on the basement floor where anything could be hidden.

On the first floor, there was a big room with side tables around a small dance floor, with a small platform at one end. In the rear were restrooms together with a small kitchen and pantry. It was quickly obvious there was no place on that floor where Arcieri's cache of goods could be stored.

On the second floor were the living quarters. Because of the slope of the roof, the bedrooms and living room had been narrowed down. In the rear were a kitchen and pantry; toward the rear, under the sloping roof on the south side, was a long clothes-press extending the full length of the house; on the north side was a bathroom with a small clothes-press which occupied only the rear or west half of the space under the slope. In the small closet, on each wall, were hung some crucifixes; under the lowest north wall was a small bureau with another small chest of drawers against the east wall. That was all. Apparently, at a casual glance, there was no room for Joe's goods.

But, as I had looked the place over before entering, I hadn't observed any dormers in the architecture of the house, and it occurred to me that on both sides of the building, under the slopes, there either had to be dormers easterly out toward the road or there had to be some concealed rooms. So I sent a deputy sheriff downstairs to go outside and see whether there were any jogs in the house where the roof slanted. He reported back that the walls were flush all the way, front to rear, on both sides.

Amid the protests and screams of the proprietor and his wife, I directed deputies to get some axes and knock out the partition over the small bureau where one of the crucifixes was hung. The proprietor and his wife, objecting strenuously, used every possible means, physical and otherwise, to stop us from doing this. They said that we were going to wreck their house and that there was no concealed room or anything else at the back of the crucifix.

The officers, however, restrained them and, after removing the crucifix, knocked out what proved to be a partition. There we beheld a narrow room, about 25 feet in length, in which was stored furniture, trunks, clothes, and furnishings of all sorts.

In the meantime, someone had reached Joe Arcieri, who came storming upstairs when we were taking out the goods from the concealed room. He protested violently and vigorously against our doing this. Accompanied by one or more of his sons, they claimed these things had been put there for storage long before the fire downtown and that the closet had been sealed over so the tenants couldn't get into them. He insisted that the tenant knew nothing about them, and apparently, he didn't. I told Joe that if that turned out to be the case. and if the goods were not connected with his fire, we would return them to him in good shape.

Under the power of the search warrant, the deputies removed the entire contents of the hidden room to the jail at Bath. There, they made a complete inventory. This inventory checked almost item for item with the detailed inventory filed with the insurance companies by Arcieri with this proof of loss.

On the basis of this concrete evidence, the next Grand Jury promptly indicted Joe for attempting to defraud an insurance company by filing a false proof of insurance loss in violation of Section 1202 of the Penal Law of the State of New York. The punishment for this was for not more than five years, a fine of $500, or both.

On arraignment before County Judge Brown, Arcieri, represented by Attorney George A. King, pleaded not guilty and was brought to trial in Bath before Judge Brown and a jury on May 10, 1934. Because of the unusual nature of the discovery of these articles under the search warrant, the case created a great deal of interest. The trial, which lasted three or four days, was largely attended, mostly by friends of Arcieri from Hornell.

Before trial, on investigating Arcieri's past, we found that he and his wife had been mixed up in a murder case some years before in or near Emporium, Pennsylvania. We anticipated that his wife, as well as other members of his family, might be witnesses for the defense. One of the trunks we had discovered in the Almond Road place was filled with costly, fancy linens and laces and wedding presents of all kinds and descriptions, as well as fancy silks and women's clothes. Another trunk was completely filled with silverware, bric-a-brac, chinaware, and fancy glassware, all very carefully packed away. A bureau dresser had expensive clothes of the finest quality stored in it. All this opulence was there in the midst of a depression.

At the trial, defense Attorney King tried to belittle the amount of goods that we had found in the speakeasy on Almond Road. As part of his defense, King claimed that many of these articles belonged to a married daughter who was not living with her parents. They had just stored them for her, pending her acquiring a permanent home.

Such a defense was so vigorously pursued that I had all of the goods taken in the raid brought into the courtroom, identified, and introduced in evidence. Then, one by one, in order to show the jury the goods were not in such small amounts as the defense attorney was claiming, I took them from the trunks and spread them around the various chairs and tables in the courtroom. The place soon looked like a department store display.

On the third day of the trial, after court had adjourned in the afternoon, it became apparent Mrs. Arcieri was going to testify. I sent Deputy Sheriffs Travis and Andrews 150 miles away to Emporium, Pennsylvania, to see what they could learn about that murder in which we had heard she was involved. The two deputies arrived in Emporium about 10:30 in the evening and hunted for the sheriff and the justice of the peace before whom the Arcieri case had first come.

At first, the sheriff and the justice didn't want to open up the courthouse at that time of night to let them see the records of the case, but after much persuasion as to the urgency of the situation, together with the persuasive power of a number of friendly drinks, the deputies were taken to the courthouse, shown the original records, and some of the evidence that had been preserved.

These, as I recall, included the murder weapon and some other things that seemed to connect Mrs. Arcieri with the alleged crime. However, she was never finally convicted.

After a great deal of coaxing, the deputies persuaded the peace justice and the sheriff to loan them those original exhibits, which, of course, were no longer necessary there because the case had been finished. These were brought back to Bath, arriving just as court was opening the following morning. A good night's work...

As anticipated, that morning, Mrs. Arcieri was the first defense witness called. In the courtroom, the spectators were a large number of friends of the Arcieri family. Mrs. Arcieri denied that she and her husband had gone to Pennsylvania so as to have the house vacant when it burned. She denied having the goods removed from the house and stored in the Almond Road house. She also denied sealing the room off with a partition for the purpose of concealing the furnishings that had been claimed as losses. She testified they had sealed it off because they were renting the place and didn't want the tenants to have access to or knowledge of the valuable things that they had stored there.

One trunk she identified as belonging to one of her sons who had been recently married. On cross-examination, I asked her particularly about this trunk. She stoutly maintained that it was "Louie's" and that all the things in there were his personal clothes and belongings. As a matter of fact, this trunk was filled with women's clothes, including what is ordinarily considered "unmentionables." Much to the amusement of the jury, I very carefully reached down into the trunk, pulled out a pair of ladies' panties, and asked her when Louie started wearing those. Of course, the audience was enjoying all this hugely, and Defense Counsel King was constantly on his feet objecting to such a demonstration. But it was obvious that she was lying about most of the details, and the judge permitted my examination to continue, overruling further objections on the grounds they bore on the witness's veracity.

When I asked her if she had ever been convicted of a crime, she said she hadn't. I then confronted her with one of the records that Deputies Travis and Andrews had procured the night before in Emporium, Pennsylvania, showing that she had been arraigned before a justice of the peace there and, at the preliminary arraignment, had pleaded guilty to homicide. She was nonplussed.

It was a dramatic moment, the courtroom was in an uproar. Defense Counsel King was making all kinds of objections and moved for a mistrial at almost every question. But this type of examination did bear directly upon her credibility as a witness, so the judge overruled the objections, and she had to testify.

It appears, however, that this plea of guilty was made during preliminary arraignment, a procedure we do not permit before a magistrate in New York State. I then showed her for identification some of the exhibits brought from Pennsylvania that had been used in the homicide case against her. She finally had to admit that these were the prosecution's exhibits in that trial and that she was involved in the murder.

It was claimed in Pennsylvania that she participated in that homicide. As I now recall it, not having the record of this case before me, on the final trial, she was not convicted, so all of this evidence was subsequently stricken out. The damage had been done, however, so far as her credibility was concerned, and she left the witness stand thoroughly discredited in the eyes and minds of the jurors.

Joe Arcieri then testified on his own behalf. He was so eager to answer questions and get his story to the jury that his own counsel had a great deal of difficulty in restraining him. Counsel constantly had to caution him to answer the questions and not volunteer information. For even an ordinary cross-examiner, a man of Arcieri's fiery and belligerent temperament was an easy mark. It was easy within a couple of minutes to wind him up into a rage so that he would pound on the railing in front of him and shake his fist at me. When the judge cautioned him about his outbursts, he shook his fist at the judge.

Finally, Arcieri jumped right off the witness stand, yelling at the top of his lungs. His counsel shouted back at him to be quiet and get back on the stand. The judge pounded his gavel to restore order, and Arcieri's friends in the audience just roared with laughter at his actions. He rushed to the railing in front of the jury, pounded on the rail, yelled at the top of his lungs, and shook his fist at some of the jurors. His counsel finally succeeded in making himself heard and requested a recess, and order was restored. Of course, during all this, I kept fanning the flames with searchingly pointed and barbed questions about Arcieri's veracity.

As soon as court resumed, with a few well-placed barbs, I wound him up again. This time, he was even worse than the first time. I caught him in so many contradictions and misstatements it was obvious no one could possibly believe his testimony in any particular. All this continued to delight his supposed friends, who were spectators at the trial. The more Arcieri raved, the more they laughed.

It took the jury only a very short time to convict him as charged. Sentencing was deferred by Judge Brown for a week. Arcieri was unable to furnish the high bail that was fixed, so he was remanded to the County Jail pending his sentence.

The following day, I received a phone call in my office in Corning from the sheriff, who said Arcieri wanted to see me right away. At the jail, in the presence of the sheriff, the undersheriff, several of the deputies, and the arson investigator, Darrow, Joe Arcieri said to me, "What am I going to do?"

"Joe, you are going to jail," I told him.

"Why should I go to jail when all those other fellows are going scot-free?" he asked.

"What other fellows?" I inquired.

"Didn't you hear them laughing at me in the courtroom during the trial?"

"Joe, they have a saying out in Chicago," I replied, "that when a crook gets into a tight situation like you are in now, he starts to 'sing', and you better start singing, just like a canary."

15
CHANGE OF VENUE

Because of the publicity and intense interest that had been shown in the trial of the first three defendants in the arson cases, the remaining nine defendants immediately moved for a Change of Venue, claiming they could not get a fair trial in Steuben County. Upon the argument of this motion, the defendants' attorneys urged that the trial be changed to Monroe County, some 75 miles from Bath where the first three defendants had been tried. Rochester, the hub of Monroe County, was a fairly large metropolitan city, and the defendants' attorneys, who lived in Rochester, thought they would have an advantage.

The Court, however, sensed the situation. Although it granted the motion, it fixed the new place of trial as Penn Yan in Yates County, which adjoins our rural county of Steuben. A veteran justice of the Supreme Court, the Honorable Willis K. Gillette, who had been a former sheriff and then county judge who had heard many criminal cases, was assigned to preside over the trials. The remaining defendants were tried in groups of three, each group being involved in an incendiary fire. The trials lasted three weeks.

These trials followed the same pattern as the first trial in Bath, and the defendants suffered the same fate. All were found guilty. Prior to the trial, one defendant pleaded guilty and testified for the people. We had ascertained that he was not directly involved in any of the incendiary fires but had gone along for the ride from Hornell to Rochester when several of the other defendants had obtained incendiary materials for their fires. He did not realize until it was too late that he was being involved in an arson case. The other eight defendants were each given the same punishment as the three who were tried in Bath; namely, 12½ to 25 years in State Prison and a $500 fine with one day of additional incarceration for each $2.00 of the fine unpaid.

Thus ended the terror that existed in the city of Hornell from the 35 incendiary fires that had so long puzzled the authorities there. Additional proof of the guilt of the ones convicted may be spelled out from the fact that for the next 25 years, there was not another incendiary fire in the city of Hornell.

16

PETTY RACKETS

During the fall of 1933, Edward Preger, proprietor of a men's clothing store in Corning and the president of the Corning Retail Men's Clothiers Association, called me on the phone and said that the members of his association would like to meet with me at my earliest convenience as they had a matter to lay before me.

I met with about a dozen of the members of the Association at the offices of the Chamber of Commerce in Corning one evening. Their spokesman told me that one of their members was illegally running a suit club. He said that this clothier had signed up a considerable number of customers at a dollar a week. The first week, and each week thereafter, the clothier would hold a drawing. The first name out of the hat would receive any suit of a certain well-advertised, moderately priced brand. The next week, another name would be drawn, and the man holding the lucky number would get a suit having paid $2, and so on. The number of men in the suit club was the same as the retail price of the particular brand of suits that was being sold. At any one time, if the retail dealer had more people than that number, he started another club; at times he would have several clubs going at the same time.

The clothiers association wanted him prosecuted for violation of the lottery section of the Penal Law, Section 1370, which reads as follows: "1370 Lottery defined – A 'lottery' is a scheme for the distribution of property by chance, among persons who have paid or agreed to pay a valuable consideration for the chance, whether called a lottery, raffle, or gift enterprise or by some other name."

Section 1371 declared a lottery to be "unlawful and a public nuisance." A violation was punishable by imprisonment of not more than two years, or by a fine of not more than $1,000, or both. The spokesman then produced a brief that had been obtained by the association from the general counsel for the National Clothiers Association in Chicago and wanted me to look it over.

I told the spokesman no brief was necessary. If the facts were as outlined, there wasn't any question: it was a violation of the Penal Law. So I said, "I will draw up an information charging him with such a violation. Which one of you gentlemen will sign it? It should be the one that has actual knowledge of all the facts."

Right away there was consternation among all those present. Not one of them wanted to place his signature on the complaint. They all maintained that not only would it subject them to the enmity of their fellow member who was violating the law, but it would harm their business all over town. One of them suggested that I sign the information. I pointed out that the one who signs this complaint must be someone who had personal knowledge of the facts.

They wanted me to get the facts and I agreed. I then pointed out to them that I had heard that there were a number of other petty rackets going on in the city of Corning and it wouldn't do to prosecute one and ignore the others. Our largest industry is the Corning Glass Works, which is world-renowned, not only for technical glass but art glass, chemical glassware, light bulbs, tubing, and many other useful glass products.

The Corning Glass Works had provided a clubhouse for its members. I told them I had heard indirectly, that contrary to this same law, there were punch boards at the clubhouse. I told the group that it wasn't fair to prosecute one petty racketeer and not the others. I said that I knew some of their members had many friends not only among the workmen of the Corning Glass Works but among the officials, and at least they should take it up with these officials before cracking down on the punch boards in the clubhouse.

Furthermore, I noticed some of the members of the Clothiers Association were members of the American Legion. The Legion, shortly before this meeting, had held a carnival in order to raise money for the local post and I had learned, indirectly, that they had wheels of chance at the carnival. I told them I felt sure that evidence could be obtained as to that violation of the law by the Legion, and I would see that the Clothiers Association got due credit for instigating the prosecution.

I also observed among the membership of the Association several members of a certain prominent church in town. This church had, several weeks before, run a bingo game. I knew about this because my small boy, age seven, had gone to the bingo game and lost 12¢. I felt that I could get other evidence to corroborate my son's statement.

I also called their attention to an automobile that just prior to this meeting had been raffled off at the Fox Theatre. Tickets for the car raffle had been obtained from local merchants, among whom were some of the members of this Association who had participated as sponsors, their names having been so listed from night to night on the theatre screen. These tickets were given out as a bonus through the purchase of merchandise. Tickets were also given by the theatre for each admission, but at the time of the drawing, the general public was not admitted. The raffle was only for ticket holders who had either purchased merchandise and held tickets or those who had been admitted to the theatre. I told them that I thought that this also might be a violation of the lottery section and that their members who had participated in this Fox Theatre automobile lottery would also have to be charged with violating the lottery law.

I also observed among the clothiers present, there were six who were members of the same fraternal organization that I belonged to. This fraternal organization not too long before had held a fair. I had stayed away from it purposely because I suspected from the undercurrent of talk that was going around that some articles were to be raffled off; I didn't want to have any personal knowledge of such a procedure. I told them I thought this evidence could be obtained. Regrettably, it would also be necessary to prosecute this fraternal organization and everyone connected therewith.

By that time, the discussion had become sharp and acrimonious, and when I insisted that one of them sign an information-complaint against the member of their Association who was running the suit club, they unanimously decided that they would withdraw the complaint.

I also pointed out to the members of this association not only what an unpopular move this would be but also how difficult it would be to draw an unbiased jury. I had no personal knowledge of these so-called violations of law; it was just general talk around town.

Then I told them about a minister from up county who had preached a sermon denouncing certain types of law violations. He accused officials of not enforcing the laws and intimated that he had knowledge of law violations. His sermon had received great publicity in the newspapers, so I promptly subpoenaed the minister before the next grand jury. He was a dud. He didn't know anything specifically, just the usual hearsay that you can pick up on any street corner. Nevertheless, we tried to run down his charges, but on such an investigation everybody runs for cover and denies any knowledge of the law violations. In other words, the great majority of people are unwilling to accept personal responsibility for initiating or even helping in crusades of this kind.

The members of the Clothiers Association walked out, sadder but wiser men. I thereupon quietly got in touch with the clothier, told him I had received a complaint against his running a suit club, without disclosing the complaint, and suggested that he quit forthwith. He did so immediately and thanked me for handling this matter in a quiet way without prosecution.

17
BOOTLEGGING

When I started as district attorney in 1932, sentiment for the repeal of the Volstead Prohibition Act was steadily building up. Franklin D. Roosevelt had made his first campaign for president, not only on the chaotic economic situation that resulted from the collapse of the stock market but with the promise of light wines and beer and the repeal of the Volstead Act. Enthusiasm for the enforcement of national prohibition was at a very low ebb, a condition that was constantly encouraged by most of the country's newspapers and magazines. Undoubtedly, they were influenced by a strong desire once again to have the lucrative liquor advertising that they missed during national prohibition. Newspapers and magazines laid heavy stress on the lack of personal freedom and responsibility that they claimed prohibition had imposed upon the country.

Bootleggers and gangsters had become tremendously powerful through their indiscriminate and utter disregard not only of the prohibition law but of all laws. Graft and corruption of public officials, police, and liquor enforcement officers were tearing down our traditional respect for law and order. Throughout the country, there were many cases of murder, robbery, hijacking, gang slayings, bribery, and perjury. They involved not only the lowest crooks but also many others who held high positions of trust and responsibility. As to liquor, generally, the public was divided between "wets," who favored liquor, and "drys," who were opposed to its sale and use. The "wets" inevitably became aligned with the bootleggers and the criminals who supplied them.

The rural areas of upstate New York were no exception to the operations of many of the would-be big-time criminals. But there were several areas that under a local option had elected to be "dry," even before the prohibition era. The village of Canisteo in the western part of Steuben County had long been dry under local option. Mrs. Rose Baker for many years had been the head of the County Women's Christian Temperance Union. She was very active in the work of that organization both before and after prohibition came into effect, and even for a number of years after its repeal. In her home village of Canisteo, she had been incensed by the open defiance of a number of small-time bootleg operators. There was no state enforcement act to back up the federal Volstead Act, and local authorities considered themselves helpless to assist in stopping bootlegging activities.

In Canisteo, one woman in particular by the name of Augusta Graves, better known as "Gussie" Graves, had several times been prosecuted, but each time she had managed to escape conviction. The violations with which she was charged as a bootlegger were usually local ordinances or disorderly conduct charges, and invariably she demanded a jury trial. The trials were held in the small Town Hall. Before the time set for the trial she would have all her drinking customers and companions, "wets," pack the place as spectators.

On several occasions, Mrs. Baker had rallied a number of women, "drys," to attend the trials, but when they arrived, the place was already packed with "wets," and her "drys" couldn't even get inside the door to attend the trial. The jurors, of course, heard the crowd's indications, which included not only smiles but laughter and applause for Gussie's case, and even shouts every time that the defense attorney scored a point. Naturally, the jurors accepted such a strong showing of public opinion, and "Gussie" Graves was found not guilty each time she had been tried.

Those unsuccessful prosecutions had all occurred before my election. But after I came into office, I decided to change the theory of prosecution and inaugurated a campaign against bootleggers. One difficulty we had, however, was that some of the county officials, as well as several members of the Board of Supervisors, liked their liquor. Hence, for some months I was unable to get the necessary funds appropriated by the Board of Supervisors. Once that hurdle was cleared, we were able to start the campaign. It involved having a "buy" man procure liquor and on the basis of that, we charged the seller with a violation of our Penal Law relating to disorderly conduct.

Section 43 of the Penal Law, which we facetiously referred to as the "Elephant's Foot," because it covered so much ground, provided a penalty for acts for which no punishment was otherwise provided. In part, Section 43 then provided:

A person who wilfully and wrongfully commits any act which seriously injures the person or property of another, or which seriously disturbs or endangers the public peace or health, or which openly outrages public decency, for which no other punishment is expressly prescribed by this chapter, is guilty of a misdemeanor.

And Section 722 of the Penal Law Involving disorderly conduct, provided that:

"Any person who with intent to provoke a breach of the peace or whereby a breach of the peace may be occasioned, commits any of the following acts shall be deemed to have committed the offense of disorderly conduct:
* * * 11. Is engaged in some illegal occupation or who bears an

evil reputation and with an unlawful purpose consorts with thieves or criminals or frequents unlawful resorts." Punishment for the violation of this section was by "imprisonment in the county jail for a term not exceeding six months, or a fine not exceeding $50.00, or by both, or by being placed on probation for a term not to exceed two years."

Even though we were hampered by the lack of any State Act for enforcing the prohibition of the sale of liquor, by proceeding under the theory that selling liquor in violation of the Federal Volstead Act was an unlawful occupation and that maintaining a place for such sale, as well as frequenting an unlawful resort, were illegal acts, we had considerable success in prosecuting the local bootleggers.

I have mentioned before in this story Sergeant Charles G. Burnett of the State Police. He lived in the village of Canisteo and had received many complaints from Mrs. Baker and her friends about Mrs. Graves' activities. On two occasions prior to my becoming district attorney, Sergeant Burnett had made complaints against Gussie, and she had been prosecuted by my predecessor, but each time she had won. My predecessor thought it was because of the pressure created by the "wets" who had attended the trials.

On discussing this situation with "Sarge," I suggested that he get a buy on Gussie and we would prosecute her again. This time, he should tell Mrs. Baker to have her group of "drys" go to the courtroom in force at least a half hour before the trial was scheduled to start and pack the place so that the "wets" would be on the outside and the "drys" on the inside.

That's exactly what Sergeant Burnett did.

Mrs. Baker had a group of more than 50 women there at 9:30 a.m. They occupied all the seats and most of the standing room in this small town hall. When the "wets" arrived for the 10:00 a.m. trial, there was no room for them.

Gussie Graves was defended by our friend Floyd Whiteman, the blind lawyer, who used every trick in the book, but to no avail in the knock-down and drag-out legal battle that this turned out to be.

The trial before the justice of the peace and a six-man jury stretched out from 10 in the morning until midnight. This time, it was the "drys" who did the clapping, laughing, and cheering.

This display of "public" interest evidently impressed the jury for they promptly convicted Gussie. The judge fined her $50.00 and put her on probation for two years. That ended her illegal activities. She didn't dare violate her probation, as she would have been incarcerated in the County Jail for six months.

18

FUN WITH THE JUDGE

One of the "buy men" we used was a young man from Bath, Stanley Fairchild, well known in the central part of the county, who was anxious to get more police experience. He afterward became a very capable deputy sheriff. One day, I decided to play a joke on Judge Brown and my friend Bill Dartt.

I said to Fairchild, "Stanley, take a run down the west shore of Lake Keuka and make as many buys as you can."

He looked at me with a twinkle in his eye and said, "You mean, stop at Bill Dartt's, too?"

"Sure," I said. "Why should we make any exception of him?"

"That's like shooting fish in a barrel," he said. "It will be a pushover."

Bill Dartt was a vineyardist by profession. Before Prohibition, Lake Keuka was, and for that matter still is, noted for the fine wines produced from the grapes grown on the hillsides surrounding the lake. With the advent of Prohibition, the grape business suffered tremendously, and a number of vineyardists made and sold wines and grape brandy surreptitiously.

At this point, I shall make a digression. Our county judge, Hon.

Edwin S. Brown, a former district attorney, was an outstanding man in the county. He was somewhat of a character, well-known, and one of our county's leading orators. He also was a fine judge in a criminal case when dealing with real criminals. But he was lenient with those who had simply been unable to withstand temptation, or had accidentally become involved in some violation of law and just needed a restraining and guiding hand, especially where youth was involved. He had strong political connections. One of his chief backers was the Hon. William W. Clark, a former justice of the Supreme Court who sat on the Appellate Division and had also been acting presiding justice of that court.

When the incumbent county judge died, Brown, then district attorney, wanted to be appointed county judge. In the normal course of events under our county's unwritten rule in the Republican Party for political advancement, all other things being equal, he would be entitled to the job. But, "all other things" were not equal.

Brown had a widely known fondness for alcoholic spirits, and for that reason alone there was considerable objection, especially among certain influential "drys." Several other candidates, therefore, entered the field to secure this appointment until an election could be held. Brown's prospects were not good.

The Hon. Nathan L. Miller, a former judge of the Court of Appeals, was then the governor and he had the power to fill the post of county judge until an election could be held. Judge Clark, who wanted to help Brown, had a tremendous state-wide acquaintanceship, and he knew Governor Miller very well. Unknown to Brown, Clark prevailed upon Governor Miller, as a personal favor, to give Brown the appointment as county judge.

After securing the governor's promise, Clark said to Brown, "Ed, I am taking a business trip to Albany, and I would like to have you go along with me." Brown had been a clerk in Clark's office at one time, and the two were great personal friends, so Brown readily acquiesced.

After they arrived in Albany, Judge Clark said, "Ed, let's go up and pay our respects to the governor. It won't do you any harm."

That night, they went to the governor's mansion. As soon as Clark introduced Brown to Miller, without any preliminaries the governor said, "Mr. Brown, I understand that you want to be county judge of your county." This kind of took Brown off his feet, but he managed to stammer, "Yes, I should like that very much."

Then the governor sternly said, "I understand you are a drinking man," and Brown, sure his goose was cooked, managed to stammer, "Yes, I-I-I-take a drink once in a while." The governor smiled and said, "So do I. What will you have?"

Judge Clark and the governor then laughed heartily, and Brown knew it was in the bag. As told to me by Judge Clark, that's the way Brown received his appointment as county judge.

To get back to our story, it was well known in select circles that Judge Brown got at least part of his personal liquor supply from Bill Dartt. Stanley Fairchild knew it as well as I did, but he never said a word, and with a knowing and sly look, he left. He went down along the west side of Lake Keuka, and without any difficulty, made six buys from vineyardists who had either known Faiarchild or knew of him. These cases I presented to the next grand jury. They were all duly indicted, including Bill Dartt.

On the day of arraignment, they were all directed to appear in County Court at 10:00 a.m. When Judge Brown stepped through the door, before taking his seat, he looked over the front row of seats where the prisoners to be arraigned were usually located. Some 25 or more were there awaiting arraignment.

When the judge spied Bill Dartt, his personal supplier, without even taking his chair, he said to the court crier, "Mr. Crier, this court will take a recess for five minutes. I would like to see the district attorney in my chambers."

In chambers, he said to me, "What's Bill Dartt doing out there with those prisoners?"

"Oh," I said, "I sent Stanley down the lake and he made a few buys, including Bill Dartt. So we indicted them all."

"You aren't going to try him before me," he declared. "Send him in here and let me talk to him."

So, I had Bill Dartt brought in and the judge said, "Bill, they tell me Stanley got a buy on you. Is that right?"

"Hell, yes," said Bill.

"Well go out there and plead guilty," said the judge, "and I will fine you like the rest of them."

"Not by a damn sight," said Bill.

"Why not?" roared Judge Brown. "You are guilty, aren't you? And you can afford to pay the fine."

"Yes, I am guilty," Bill said, "and I don't care about the fine, but it's the humiliation of getting caught."

"Never mind the humiliation," roared the judge, "You get out there and plead guilty and pay your fine like the rest of them."

Bill went out and pleaded guilty along with the others, and the judge fined each one $100.

All of us who knew of the situation had a lot of laughs and chuckles.

Afterward, I felt pretty badly at having pulled this joke on the judge and also on Bill Dartt, because I had known Bill and grown up with his son, Alvah. My family had a summer cottage near the Dartt home on Lake Keuka. I figured, however, that someday I would repay both of them. I repaid Judge Brown many times over in various ways in our association while I was district attorney, but it was not until three years later after I had become judge of the Surrogate's Court that the chance to repay BIll Dartt came along.

At the opening of the June term of the Supreme Court in Bath in 1936, I happened to be in the courthouse, which was close to where I was holding Surrogate's Court. There I met two Federal Prohibition agents whom I had known and worked with when I was district attorney but hadn't seen for some months. They were in the lobby of the courthouse near where the grand jury was in session. After passing the time of day with them, I asked, "What brings you down here, grand jury?"

One of them said, "No, we have a line on a couple of buys along the lake and are going down to knock them off."

After that, I hastened back to the Surrogate's Court. My deputy clerk at that time was Edwin F. Smith, son of Supreme Court Judge Edwin C. Smith. They had a summer cottage on Lake Keuka within a stone's throw of Bill Dartt's place. It was a beautiful day in June, and I knew that the Smith family at that time was staying at the lake and that Eddie was commuting back and forth. "Ed," I said, "How would you like to have the day off to go down to the lake? It is a beautiful day."

"I would love it," he said.

"Well, climb in your car and get going. Do it fast and stop off at Bill Dartt's and tell him that the 'Feds' are in town."

"How do you know?" he asked.

I said, "Never mind how I know or how I suspect what might happen, but Bill will know what to do. Don't under any circumstances tell Bill where you got your tip."

So Eddie hurried out, drove some fifteen miles down the lake, and gave Bill Dartt my message.

Bill was a big, powerful man about 6'2", and weighed 230 or 240 pounds. But he had a heart condition and, at that particular time, he was alone at his home when Eddie arrived. His cellar contained a considerable stock of wine and brandy. Bill's vineyard was alongside and in back of his house on a very steep hill that ran right down to the lakeshore. All alone, he started carrying his liquor supply some distance back up the steep hill into the vineyard rows. It was almost too much for such a heavy man with a bad heart condition. But he managed to transfer all but two jugs of his liquor supply into the vineyard hideaway. In fact, with those two one-gallon jugs, he had to sit down on his steps to catch his breath.

Just then, the Federal agents drove up and all they could find was an exhausted Bill and two one-gallon jugs of wine. They confiscated them, placed him under arrest, and in due time he was indicted and arraigned in Federal Court in Elmira, New York, for violation of the Volstead Act. Because all he had was the two one-gallon jugs, the federal judge fined him only $50, even though this was Bill's third offense in Federal Court.

Bill figured he was pretty lucky to be let off, but it was not for years until he finally found out who furnished the tip-off information to Eddie Smith.

I think I repaid Bill for the joke I played on him and Judge Brown. I found out later that he and Judge Brown had enjoyed many laughs over the incident.

19
DISAPPEARING EVIDENCE

During Prohibition, the city of Corning, with a population of 16,000, was not without its bootleggers. Because of its cosmopolitan nature, getting convictions in Corning City Court was much more difficult than it was in some of the dryer rural areas. Corning City Court had jurisdiction of cases of this kind, which some of the justices of the peace of towns did not have. Cases, therefore, could be brought before the city judge on information rather than by a grand jury's indictment. Invariably, the defendants demanded a jury trial.

In all of these cases, it was necessary not only to swear in the "buy man" as to his purchase of liquor but his buy had to be carefully labeled, sealed, and dated. Every person who had handled it had to be sworn in to identify the bottle. Tags would be secured complete with the person's initials and the date when he handled it. It is called the Chain of Evidence.

The contents had to be analyzed by a chemist, and they had to have an alcoholic content of +3.5% by volume. Usually, we also swore in one of the officers who had some knowledge of liquor from personal experience. He could testify that he had tested it, that he was familiar with liquor, and that in his opinion this was liquor that was satisfactory to drink. When the case was finally submitted, in order to impress the jury, we usually left the buy bottle with the jury so that they could observe it as to color and odor.

In one particular case in Corning City Court, the jury found the defendant not guilty. After the jury left, we looked at the bottle placed in evidence, which was supposed to have contained the liquor that had been bought. We found not a drop. The bottle was empty.

One juror, the foreman, had polished off the entire contents. He announced to the other jurors that it was not intoxicating, so the jury acquitted the defendant. We were informed afterward that each juror in turn had taken a sip of the liquor, but the foreman drank the rest of the bottle, rather like a priest who at the end of Communion finishes off the transubstantiated wine. The foreman appeared perfectly sober as he announced the verdict.

Abb W. Eckess had been a New York Central Railroad detective. Prior to that, he had been a Pennsylvania state trooper for a number of years, and before that a cavalryman in the Regular Army of the United States, with extensive service in the Philippines. In between, he also had a security job in Washington, D.C. So, he was eminently qualified to take over the duties of chief of police of the city of Corning.

During his service as a railroad detective, a certain Corning man had given Eckess all kinds of trouble. For obvious reasons here I shall call him John Doe because since that time this man has reformed and become a good citizen of the city of Corning. He had been engaged extensively in bootlegging operations, and together with others he formed a gang that began stealing from New York Central Railroad cars on a large scale.

Their scheme to steal merchandise that was being transported by the Railroad was to break open the seals of the cars just after the train was slowly starting out from the yards, scramble aboard, and throw the merchandise out along the side of the railroad track while the train was moving away. Then others of the gang would quickly collect the goods, haul them away, and sell them.

Eckess had caught Doe and some of his pals and prosecuted them. He had more or less broken that ring at about the time he became chief of police of Corning. Doe, however, then resumed his car-rifling activities and began to swap the stolen goods for alcohol. Then he mixed up "bathtub gin" from the alcohol, which he sold at a nice profit. His bootlegging operations became a thorn in the side of Chief Eckess, who was trying hard to maintain a good, clean city.

At one time, Doe had conspired with two other local toughs to try to kill Eckess, but that conspiracy never was carried out. The two other law-breakers were arrested for other crimes before they could set up and carry out the murder.

When I became district attorney, Chief Eckess told me the story and of his earnest desire to put Doe out of business, but Doe had seemed to anticipate his every move. I suggested to Eckess that even though he didn't have an airtight case if he had strong suspicions that Doe was transporting alcohol in order to make it up into the "bathtub gin" that was very popular in Prohibition days, he could arrest him and we could prosecute him anyway. This would compel him to hire a lawyer, an expense he wasn't counting on and hadn't factored into his "overhead." We would cause him every bit of expense and legal trouble we could and would continue to do so, again and again until at least his bootlegging operations would cease to be profitable.

Chief Eckess agreed to this, and when he had pinpointed the routes that Doe was taking to run his alcohol into Corning, he called Sergeant Burnett of the State Police and asked him if he would try to catch Doe in a traffic violation at a time when he was transporting the illicit alcohol in his car. Then because there had been a violation of law, he could legally search his car and that evidence would stand up in court.

Sergeant Burnett immediately stationed a couple of troopers at a stop sign intersection along one of Doe's routes on a night when it was suspected Doe would be transporting some of his alcohol. The troopers saw Doe going through the stop sign, immediately nabbed him, and found two gallons of alcohol and a blackjack in his car. We felt we then had a solid case against him.

Doe got out on bail while his case was pending, and Chief Eckess and Sergeant Burnett began talking to him about going straight and trying to make a man out of himself. The chief knew his family and felt sorry for them.

On Doe's promise to go straight, the chief got him a job in the Corning Glass Works, where he had worked before. He was a good workman when he wasn't engaged in these other operations. His work was in a department that was under the supervision of a very prominent citizen, James P. Hallahan, who had been mayor of Corning and who was a friend of the Eckess. Doe had no more than started to work when some straw boss under Hallahan, knowing of Doe's bad criminal record, immediately fired him.

Doe came to Chief Eckess in a rage and said, "What's the use of going straight; I got that job in the Glass Works with every intent of reforming and doing just as you and Sergeant Burnett urged me to do. When this straw boss found out about my being there and knowing my bad record, he fired me. It will always be that way. If I can't have the chance to earn an honest living, I have got to earn a dishonest one."

Chief Eckess immediately called Jim Hallahan and told him the situation. Hallinan overruled the straw boss and put Doe right back to work, and there he stayed.

When the Doe case finally came up for disposition and it was shown that he was rehabilitating himself and seemed in earnest about his promises, Judge Brown suspended the jail sentence, placed him on probation, and fined him only $50. That was way back in 1932, and Doe has continued to work for the Glass Works and gone straight ever since.

This man had gotten in with bad companions in his youth. He was well on his way toward being a confirmed criminal when he found he couldn't make an honest living even though he wanted to. He would have always been a criminal if a kind-hearted chief of police hadn't gone to bat for him and rescued him in the nick of time.

As a further illustration of how unpopular the enforcement of the Federal Volstead Prohibition Act was, I am reminded of an incident that occurred while I was district attorney, but I was not directly concerned with it. In the city of Hornell, there was a large brewery known as the Schwarzenbaugh Brewery. Federal enforcement agents had secured evidence that the prohibition law was being violated by illegal withdrawals of beer from the brewery. Through a federal padlock proceeding, the Feds closed the brewery. To enforce this padlock proceeding, they stationed three Federal officers there. They were to stand guard in shifts around the clock to see that the brewery didn't dispose of any of its beer.

One night, someone dropped in to see one of the Federal agents and found all of them dead drunk. They were so drunk they couldn't talk. The friend took them in a car back to the hotel where they were living and sobered them up overnight. That left the brewery unguarded, but fortunately, no one else knew of this, and there were no illegal withdrawals that night.

When Federal agents themselves were guilty of such performances, one can readily see that Prohibition itself was unpopular and why it didn't get the enthusiastic enforcement to which all laws are entitled. Clearly, not only was the Prohibition law unpopular with the citizenry, but also the temptations that these Federal enforcement agents were constantly subjected to sometimes proved to be too much to resist.

I am mindful of a story that a fellow district attorney of one of the other counties in our Seventh Judicial District told me after he had become a Supreme Court justice. It seems that Federal agents had made buys and raids on a bootleg establishment in the city of Auburn. Under the usual and necessary practice, each bottle buy was labeled and marked with the agent's initials or name and sealed with sealing wax so as to be whole and identifiable as trial evidence.

One of the agents involved in one of these raids in Auburn lived near my home city, Corning. He was supposedly a substantial, outstanding citizen and was one of my close personal friends. He and the other agents involved in the raids were charged with having accepted bribe money to suppress the evidence and they were caught at it. They were indicted and scheduled for trial. On a change of venue, the case against them was moved and scheduled to be tried in Albany.

The D.A. had a fondness for an occasional drink of liquor himself. The night before the trial

was to begin, he had met some friends who, contrary to the D.A.'s desires and better judgment, insisted on showing him the sights of Albany. They took him into one of the very popular "speakeasies" where, to his dismay, he saw one of the defense attorneys in the next day's trial.

Once the jury had been selected and the case opened by the district attorney, the sealed bottles of liquor that bore identifying marks of these defendant agents were brought in and placed on the prosecutor's table to be later identified and offered into evidence.

When the court took a brief recess, the district attorney and other court attendants left the courtroom to go to the men's room. Through an oversight, these bottles were left unguarded on the district attorney's table. However, the D.A. returned unexpectedly. From the doorway, he saw the Federal Prohibition agent who was my personal friend sneak up to his table, grab the bottle that bore his identification marks on the cork, put the cork in his mouth, bite it, and swallow the cork along with the identifying paper and sealing wax!

Unfortunately, the D.A. didn't want to become involved. When he saw the agent destroy the admissibility of the evidence, it occurred to him instantly that if he personally made an issue of it and started an investigation, the defense attorney would tell of the D.A.'s trip to the speakeasy the night before. So the D.A. quietly slipped out of the courtroom and watched the guilty Federal Agent sneak out another door.

Because the evidence against this particular agent was gone, the case against him was dismissed. He was fired from the service, but afterward became one of our county's prominent enforcement officers. At that time, no one in our county knew about the affair, and few have known of it since. He and that D.A. are now dead, so I am violating no confidence by reporting the events here, The ensuing investigation failed to disclose who had destroyed the evidence, so the D.A.'s hide was saved but with no credit to him. Greediness for quick and easy money was just too much for a good many of those poorly paid Federal enforcement officers.

20

A VALUABLE LESSON

One valuable lesson I learned as a fledgling lawyer stood me in good stead, not only as a prosecutor but in all my rather extensive civil trial practice. It was ten years before I became district attorney,

My brother-in-law, who preceded me as district attorney, prosecuted a murder case in which the defense was insanity. Early in the proceedings, the D.A. had the local health officer, Dr. Frank S. Swain, make a preliminary examination of the accused. Dr. Swain, as the local health officer, was usually called on to examine those in the city of Corning who were candidates to be sent to state mental hospitals. By virtue of such examinations and his long service as the health officer, he had considerable experience in the mental health field. Dr. Swain reported to the D.A. that in his opinion the accused was perfectly sane at the time the crime was committed.

The defense raised the issue of insanity and demanded an examination by their experts. The D.A. retained three of the outstanding alienists in this section of the state and country. They included three of the heads of our state mental institutions. One of them had testified as an expert witness in the famous Harry K. Thaw insanity murder trial in which insanity was the defense. The defense also had three outstanding alienists, two of whom were heads of other state mental hospitals and one of whom was a private psychiatrist of national repute, especially when it came to testifying in trials, both civil and criminal, where insanity or competency was the issue. The D.A. then arranged for examinations by all of the experts. Dr. Swain was present and participated in these examinations.

When the case came to trial, I, as a young lawyer, was intensely interested in this legal battle involving mental experts. During all of their testimony, I sat in the courtroom, spellbound with open mouth, listening to the examinations and cross-examinations of these six noted expert witnesses who testified at length about the insanity or sanity of the accused. For the defense, in response to a long, hypothetical question in which the astute defense attorneys set forth all of the matters involved in the case, especially those that were favorable to the defense theory, each one of the three defense experts testified that in his opinion the defendant was insane at the time the murder was committed.

They were testifying under the narrow limitations of the so-called "McNaughten Rule" about insanity, concerning which today, in these enlightened times [1965], there is much criticism and agitation for change due to the broader views that psychiatrists now have toward acts of this character. This narrow McNaughten rule decreed a person sane if, at the time of the commission of the crime, he knew the nature and quality of the act and he knew the act he was doing was wrong.

In rebuttal, each of the three prosecution experts was asked a similar long, hypothetical question by the D. A., outlining the case as it appeared most favorable to him. With equal positiveness, each one testified in his opinion that the accused was sane.

The examinations and cross-examinations of these six experts took more than three days. I was enthralled with the whole procedure. Each side attacked the other side's hypothetical question and gave very persuasive reasons why they were mistaken. I wondered how in the world any jury could arrive at a decision when six such eminent men, really the best that the country had in the field of psychiatry and mental diseases, were in a stand-off. Three against three, and absolutely contradictory opinions and judgments as to the defendant's sanity or insanity.

Because of the long time that these examinations and cross-examinations had taken, the D.A. initially decided not to bother calling Dr. Swain, a mere local physician. He felt that these outstanding experts had covered the field; that after such profound analyses and displays of medical and psychiatric erudition, the jury wouldn't pay much attention to just a small-town local man who had nowhere near the advanced training and experience of these six experts. But he happened to look around and saw Dr. Swain, who had sat patiently through the three days of expert examinations, waiting to be called.

He thought to himself, *If I don't call Dr. Swain, his feelings would be terribly hurt.* So he put Dr. Swain on the stand and rather hurriedly and briefly brushed him off with questions about his qualifications as a physician and health officer. Dr. Swain then testified quickly that he had heard all the experts' testimony, that he had a copy of the hypothetical question asked of the three prosecution alienists, and that he had heard it read three times in court. The D.A. then asked, "Do you have an opinion with a reasonable degree of medical certainty, based on your own examination of this man and on the hypothetical question, as to whether the defendant was sane or insane?"

Dr. Swain promptly said he did have such an opinion. "What is that opinion?" asked the district attorney.

"He was perfectly sane at the time of the commission of this crime and is now."

"That is all," said the district attorney. "Your witness."

"No questions," said the defense attorneys. They, too, thought in view of the big-name experts that, considering the tremendous prestige and standing of the six experts who had already testified, Doc Swain couldn't possibly carry much weight with the jury.

The jury found the defendant guilty of murder in the second degree. I was eager to get the reaction of the jury, some of whom I knew quite well, to these great medical experts. So, as they were filing out of the courtroom, I spoke to several and asked them what they thought of this great array of medical and psychiatric talent that had been brought in and paraded before them at length. One of them spoke up and said, "Oh, we didn't pay any attention to them; Doc Swain said he was sane. We know Doc Swain and that was good enough for us."

I never forgot that lesson. The reaction of jurors in such cases is to believe the people that they deal with and know personally, especially when they are sound, solid, respected citizens and able physicians like Dr. Swain was in this community. For years he had lived and practiced and raised a family in the community and had participated in all of the usual fine, civic enterprises that a community of this kind has.

21

MOB PSYCHOLOGY

The city of Hornell was largely a railroad town, but it had several silk mills. Each of these mills had from three to four hundred employees. In the fall of 1934, about 300 workers at the Merrill Silk Hosiery Company went on strike. When negotiations for settlement of the strike failed, the company announced it was going to move one of its knitting machines out to another company mill, which was about 25 miles away in Allegany County. This announcement incensed the strikers, even though most of them believed that the company was bluffing. The company was not bluffing, however, and the tense feelings between the striking employees and the employers grew more and more bitter.

The striking union had notified its national headquarters, which sent a number of men to Hornell to map out a strategy for the strikers and conduct the strike negotiations. The company proceeded to dismantle one of the large knitting machines, which was some 40 feet in length. They loaded it onto a flat car of the Shawmut railway, a small line that skirted the edge of Hornell and then switched to a spur running into the mill. While the machine was being loaded onto the railroad car, crowds of strikers had gathered and threatened violence, but factory guards and local police broke up the mob gathering.

Once the knitting machine was loaded, the company pulled the car out onto a switch near the passenger and freight station. A freight train was due in two days. It would pick up the flat car and transport the machine to its destination.

The second night, while the flat car was still on the switch, some person or persons unknown at that time, threw kerosene or coal oil over the machinery, touched it off, and ran from the scene. At that time, of course, the machine was in the care and custody of the Shawmut railroad, and before the blaze could be put out by the railroad men and the Hornell fire department, the heat of the flames had totally wrecked the machine. The area fairly reeked with the oil fumes. There was no question; it was arson.

Near the scene, the local police found several empty five-gallon cans that had recently held coal oil. Beyond that, they had little to go on, except they were morally certain this fire had been touched off either by strikers or their sympathizers. Among the men that union headquarters had sent in were George Hoyt from Trenton, New Jersey, and Alexander Fellberg from Clifton, New Jersey.

Chief of Police Clarence Bailey and several of his officers, working in collaboration with Deputy Sheriff Howard M. Travis who lived in Hornell, planted dictaphones in the hotel rooms of the out-of-town strikebreakers, but without results.

Soon, the officers, through the usual scraps of information that they picked up from informers, came to the conclusion that the guilty ones were included in a small group of strikers that was often seen in the company of Hoyt and Fellberg.

Deputy Travis prevailed upon a friend of his, who also knew several of the members of this small group, to invite one of the weaker men in the group to go out for dinner, show him a good time, and buy him some drinks. This he did on several occasions over a period of several weeks. Finally, with the aid of considerable liquor, he induced the man to talk.

Enough of the story was obtained to enable police authorities to determine that four men, namely George Hoyt, Alexander Fellberg, Leo Didas, and Ralph Collier, were the ones who planned and actually did touch off the knitting machinery fire on the railroad car as it sat on the switch near the Shawmut railway station.

Chief Bailey and Deputy Travis then detained Collier, the man they thought was the weakest-willed of the four, and finally, through persistent questioning, broke him down so that he gave them the details of the whole job. On the basis of his confession, the four were indicted for arson third-degree and for conspiracy by a grand jury sitting in Hornell. Collier pleaded guilty on arraignment.

The others, Hoyt, Fellberg, and Didas, however, pleaded not guilty and were released on $2,500 bail each. When their trial came up in March 1935, however, they changed their pleas to guilty. Judge Brown, in County Court, thereupon fined them $2,000 restitution money to be paid to the railroad and gave them suspended sentences.

The lightness of the sentence was undoubtedly due to the very strong feeling in Hornell and vicinity of sympathy for the strikers and also to the fact that the four were undoubtedly carried away with an excess of zeal and enthusiasm on behalf of their striking group, many of whom were morally, if not legally, guilty of this same crime and equally responsible therefore. It was generally felt that a good many of the strikers were actually involved in the plot, but it was impossible to prove that. These four were only the mob's active agents and emissaries.

The foregoing shows how easy it is for angry men who think they have just grievances and that their jobs are threatened to be worked into a fevered pitch or frenzy, and when overcome by the emotions do something evil that in more sober moments they wouldn't consider doing at all.

22

SNEAKY LITTLE TRICKS DON'T PAY

Very late one evening in the early spring of 1933, a merchant on the northside of Corning, Robert G. Cruttenden, who ran a little gift shop on Bridge Street and whose home was nearby on West Pulteney Street, noticed something shadowy moving in the Keenan Drug Store, which was located not far from his shop on the northeast corner of Bridge and Pulteney Streets. Cruttenden realized that under ordinary circumstances there would be no one in the drug store at that time of night.

To satisfy his curiosity, he started to walk toward the store. When he saw two men sneak out the side door, he quickened his pace. The two men broke into a run. He chased them on Bridge Street to the next block where they disappeared easterly, around the corner of Bridge and Ontario, behind an old, red brick church. Crittenden was unable to find them.

He immediately found the officer on the beat, William Jones, who called headquarters and reported the incident. The investigation then disclosed that Crittenden was probably correct, and he then called the proprietor. Soon, they ascertained that among other things the vending machine for United States postage stamps had been smashed, and stamps and whatever coins were in the machine had been removed. Officer Jones earlier that evening had seen one John Foster in the vicinity. Foster, he recalled, had served a prior term for Grand Larceny in Auburn's State Prison. Immediately, word was sent out from headquarters to pick up Foster. When a known criminal is seen in the vicinity of a crime, to a police officer it is like a green traffic light, viz, the signal to move.

Chief Eckess sent Officers Fleet, Jones, Hammond, and Rose out to scour the bars and restaurants. In the Leo Ross Restaurant on Market Street, they learned that John Foster and a companion, Leon Waters, had spotted one of the officers going by the window, and they hurriedly left the restaurant. They had hastily paid for their refreshments with a handful of change. In their haste, they had dropped some of their nickels and pennies on the floor, together with some new stamps, which had obviously come from a stamp machine. Then, the officers immediately took charge of the coins and stamps, and within a very short time, they apprehended both of the fleeing men.

Further investigation disclosed that the stamps the officers found on the floor at the restaurant were unusual. Although there were other stamp-vending machines in the city, in all the others the stamps were attached by side-to-side perforations. In the vending machines at the Keenan Drug Store, the stamps were attached end to end. The stamps picked up in the restaurant right under the stools where Foster and Waters had been sitting were attached end to end. If purchased or stolen in the city of Corning, they could only have come from the Keenan machine.

When they were brought to headquarters, an officer asked each culprit to empty his pockets and lay all the contents on the desk in front of him. Each one had in his pockets a few single dollar bills, several handfuls of change, and perforated roll stamps attached end to end. From Foster's pocket, there were three one-dollar bills laid on the desk. The officer gave Foster a receipt for them and the other change and stamps.

Just then, the officer had to turn his back to answer the telephone. When he turned back to face Foster, the three one-dollar bills were gone from the desk. Having had prior dealings with Foster, the officer immediately made him disrobe and found three $1 bills tucked into Foster's shoe. If he hadn't found them, the officer would have had to account to Foster for the three dollars when Foster checked out.

Cruttenden, having arrived at police headquarters, promptly identified both Foster and Waters as the two men who had come out of Keenan's Drug Store and had run up the street. Although his identification was positive, at Foster's trial, defense counsel tried to make much of the uncertainty of positive identification on such a dark night. But there was a street light within 60 feet of the side entrance and another street light at the corner of Ontario and Bridge where they turned by the church when Cruttenden was chasing them. And Cruttenden was quite sure of his identification. He furthermore testified he had seen both of them earlier in the evening wearing the same rough-looking work clothes.

They were brought to trial in Bath on May 3, 1933. Waters then pleaded guilty and testified for the people. Foster, who had more to lose because he would be a second offender, was vigorously defended by George A. King, but the jury found him guilty anyway. Waters was given one to four years in Auburn State Prison and Foster, because of his prior conviction for grand larceny second, was given ten years in the same institution.

Foster's sneaky trick of trying to hide the three dollar bills in his shoe didn't sit well with the jury as could be sensed at the trial. Smart, and even brilliant, criminals sometimes little realize the importance of such apparently innocuous, sneaky little things. Oftentimes, as in this instance, they turned out to be the deciding factor with a jury in distinguishing guilt from innocence.

23
PARKER MURDER

While the arson cases were being tried in Penn Yan, which is about 30 miles from Bath, on Monday evening, December 17, 1934, Mrs. George H. Parker, a respected widow of about 72 years of age, was found dead in the front living room of her home, brutally clubbed to death. She lived alone in a rather large old-fashioned home on West Morris Street in the Village of Bath. Wife of a former Bath mayor, Mrs. Parker had taken an intense interest in the lives and affairs of some of the younger people of Bath. As soon as the authorities were notified, Sheriff Fred A. Cornell, Sergeant Burnett of the State Police, and their staff were all summoned and they jointly commenced an investigation.

Mrs. Parker had been found by a neighbor, Joseph Ormsby, that Monday evening lying dead in the living room with her head bashed in from what appeared to be a blackjack or piece of pipe. Blood was in a pool all around her. On the floor and walls could be seen streaks of blood where the murder instrument (which the murderer afterward told us was a "sap") had swished back and forth while striking her. We hastily set up quarters in her dining room from which to conduct the investigation. We rounded up all of the neighbors, the young friends of Mrs. Parker who had been known to visit her from time to time, and several men who had worked for her tending the furnace and caring for the lawn.

Hastily, I questioned each one of them for some preliminary details. They were naturally nervous and upset by this terrible tragedy. After I finished questioning each of them, one of the officers would take them aside and, now that the pressure was off, casually engage them in more extensive conversation. They did not realize that this was standard police procedure and would produce much more information than could be obtained by me under the pressure that existed in the wake of such a bloody tragedy.

In this way, we interviewed some 25 or 30 people that night. Among them, one was a man by the name of Joseph Lewandowski who was a World War I veteran staying at the Soldiers Home, situated about a mile away from the scene of the murder. Lewandowski was at that time Mrs. Parker's janitor and handyman. He was a near-sighted, nervous individual of low intelligence, and he seemed greatly relieved when I had finished questioning him. Sergeant Burnett then took him aside and talked with him casually about many things. Among other things, he asked Lewandowski, "What do you do up at the Home to occupy your time when you are not working?"

"The boys play cards and swap stories," replied Lewandowski. "They also walk downtown and visit the speak-easies. Also, I like to fish and snatch frogs."

"Where do you do this?" asked the sergeant.

"Up along the Cohocton River which runs close to the Veterans' Home."

Then Sergeant Burnett inquired much more into his fishing and frog snatching. Lewandowski appeared much more at ease; he talked freely and at length. Nothing more was thought of for a few days.

This investigation lasted all night. In the morning, we drove to Penn Yan to continue the arson cases, leaving a skeleton staff to continue investigating the murder in Bath. After court adjourned in Penn Yan at 5:00, we all hurried back the 30 miles to Bath to work on the investigation for the rest of that night.

In the meantime, I had called in investigator Albert Hamilton, whom I have mentioned in other places in this book. Hamilton originally had been a pharmacist in Auburn, New York. He had studied criminology until he was considered an expert in almost every branch of that inexact science, including fingerprints, chemicals, poisons, comparisons of bullets under a high-powered comparison microscope, the effects that bullets fired from revolvers, rifles, and shotguns, have upon entering various substances, handwriting, typewriting, and many other fields of criminal investigation. He was thought by some to be rather a "quack," yet he was a very adroit and resourceful investigator, a remarkably skilled and convincing witness, and a very difficult man to break down on cross-examination. Because defense attorneys in this area and many other places in the United States were apt to retain him early in a criminal case, I hired him to keep him out of my hair and avoid the possibility of his being a defense witness should the murderer ever be apprehended and this case come up for indictment or trial. He worked independently from the sheriff's officers and the State Police.

For three days and nights, we made little or no progress. Hamilton pointed out, from the blood spots and spatters on the floor, walls, and furniture, the number of times that the murderer had bludgeoned Mrs. Parker. He could determine the direction of each stroke from the position of the teardrop formations of the streaks of blood spots. In the meantime, we, who were trying the arson cases in Penn Yan, were without sleep except for "cat naps" that we were able to snatch by changing drivers while traveling back and forth. This lasted for 72 hours.

One of the things that puzzled us was the fact that Mrs. Parker had apparently been reading the Sunday *Elmira Telegram*, a newspaper widely circulated in this area. It always carried a comic section, and we noticed that the funny papers section of the paper was absent. Of course, it could have been because for some reason none was included in the paper or because someone had removed it from the living room before the discovery of the body. This fact was given some publicity in our local papers.

The fourth day after the murder, while we were still engaged in trying the arson case in Penn Yan, a boy, Wilson Rahl, was skating on the river between Mrs. Parker's home and the Veterans' Home. As he was about to go home, his skate struck an object in the ice. "Just for curiosity," he skated back. The object was wrapped in a portion of "the funny papers" and tied up with a piece of fish line. He had read about the absence of the comic section of the newspaper at the murder scene and thought this object might be important. The paper was torn where his skate struck it. He noticed how blood-soaked the object was, and upon examining it more closely he found it matted with blood and long, gray hairs. "I thought it might have some connection with the Parker case," he reported.

Young Rahl took it at once to the police headquarters where it was turned over to the sheriff and investigator Hamilton. They carefully unwrapped the object and found it was a homemade, blood-stained blackjack or sap made by melting lead and pouring it into the piece of rubber hose.

I was immediately notified by phone in Penn Yan of this find and got an early adjournment of the arson case, then hastened back to Bath. When I arrived, Investigator Hamilton had carefully removed the rubber hose from the lead and examined it under a powerful microscope. He had found it bore gouges as if it had been whittled with a nicked, dull knife. I examined the fish line and found it was an old oiled silk line. It was fairly rotten, with both ends frayed as if it had been broken, rather than cut.

Deputy Sheriffs Travis and Andrews, who had been assigned to my office and who were engaged in the arson case, Sergeant Burnett, and several other troopers—all had just assembled in the sheriff's office when I arrived. When they saw the fish line, Sergeant Burnett looked at Travis and each exclaimed, "Lewandowski! Fishing!"

Burnett, Travis, Andrews, and several troopers immediately went to the Soldiers' Home to bring Lewandowski down for further questioning.

Not finding him in his quarters, several officers went out on the extensive Soldiers' Home grounds. Some officers remained in the barracks waiting for the others to find him. They saw Lewandowski's locker open at his bedside. Looking inside, they found coils of fish line, both new and old, and an old jackknife. These they borrowed, and when Lewandowski was found, he identified the fish line and jackknife as his. He was then brought down for further questioning.

Investigator Hamilton on opening the jack knife saw it had nicks in the blade. He immediately sent for a piece of solder, which he scraped with the nicked jack knife, and then compared the knicks on the fresh lead of the solder with the knicks and scraped lines on the lead of the blackjack that he had removed from the rubber hose part of the sap. Under the comparison microscope, they matched exactly, like two bullets from the same gun.

Further, Hamilton took the fish line and examined the ends under a powerful microscope. He found that the frayed strands from one of the pieces taken from Lewandowski's locker fitted and joined exactly with one end of one of the fish lines removed from the package that the boy had found on the ice. The comic paper that contained the blackjack was a portion of the Sunday *Telegram* of the same date as the paper at the scene of the murder. We immediately questioned Lewandowski at length. Without going into details of the lengthy questioning, we used every means of persuasion that we knew to get a confession that, morally certain, we felt was justified.

The rubber hose part of the sap was taken to Dr. Rudolph Shafer, our county pathologist, who determined that the blood group of AB matched that of the murdered woman. The blood spots on Lewandowski's pants and shirt were also determined to be AB.

The weather had moderated and, in fact, became very warm. In our questioning, we had brought Lewandowski, we believed, almost to the verge of a confession. But a roaring thunderstorm broke and the lights went out in the jail at that critical moment. A tree had been struck by lightning and a limb had fallen on a wire, thus causing the blackout.

When lights were restored, Lewandowski had recovered his poise. We could see that he was not going to "break" that night, so we held him for further questioning the next night. In the meantime, he had been advised of his rights but said he did not want a lawyer because he was not guilty.

The next night, after returning from trying the arson case in Penn Yan, which we finished that afternoon, we questioned him again. He still stoutly maintained that he was not guilty, but he told many lies and contradicted himself repeatedly. We, therefore, played one of the oldest police tricks in the book on him. Deputy Sheriff Travis took him into another room.

He started to raise his voice and accused Lewandowski. He finally pretended to get angry with Lewandowski, grabbed him by the coat, and started to shake him. Lewandowski started to yell. Travis demanded that he stop lying and tell the truth.

Just then, Sergeant Burnett, amid the turmoil and confusion, broke open the door, grabbed Travis, and threw him out of the office. Burnett then put his arm around Lewandowski, who had started to cry, and told him that the State Police wouldn't stand for the rough treatment displayed by the sheriff's office. He told Lewandowski that the troopers were there to protect suspects from such treatment and would see that he was protected and no harm came to him. Having won Lewandowski's confidence by comforting him very quietly, Burnett got him to admit some of his lies and suggested to him how much better it would be to end his troubles and tell the whole truth.

Lewandowski then broke down and said, "Bring in the district attorney, and I will tell him the whole story." Which he did.

It was a sordid tale. Some of it, we already knew, and it was not exactly true. But it was enough.

Lewandowski told how on one of his fishing trips, with a stick he had bored a hole in the sand on the river bank. The stick just fit inside the piece of rubber hose that he had. He melted some old lead in a tin can over a bonfire and poured it into the hole, which he used for a mold. But once the melted lead hardened in the hole, the rod of lead didn't quite fit the rubber hose. It was a little too big around. So he whittled it with his old, nicked jack knife until it fit. He identified the knife as the one he used. He then forced the lead into the rubber hose and made it into the blackjack, which he called a sap. He told us how he had made advances to Mrs. Parker, but she had turned him down, and it was for that reason he had become enraged and sapped her.

He described how he noticed the newspaper lying around there and how he picked up the comic section of the Sunday paper, wrapped the sap in it, and tied it up with a piece of fish line that he had taken from his pocket. He said, "The fish line was too long and it was kind of rotten so I broke it off and put the rest back in my pocket. It's a piece of one of those taken from my locker. Then I left the house and went up Morris Street over to the railroad and along the railroad, which runs by the river. When I had gotten a little way from the house and buildings, I threw the sap out onto the river, not realizing that it had frozen over."

He did not seem ashamed or penitent about the attempted criminal assault on her, which he described, nor about his killing of Mrs. Baker. He simply said, "I must have lost my head."

He was promptly charged with murder and shortly thereafter indicted. The court assigned an attorney for him who immediately indicated that the defense would be insanity. We had him examined by several alienists who reported that while he was definitely sane, he was of low-grade mentality and emotionally disturbed. After a number of further mental examinations and many consultations with his counsel, he pleaded guilty to first-degree manslaughter and was sent to the State Institute for Male Defective Delinquents at Napanoch, New York, where I understand he was confined for the rest of his life.

An alert officer, in remembering the apparent irrelevant talk about fishing with one of those questioned the night of the murder and relating it to the fish line which was tied around the comic section of the *Elmira Telegram*, thus solved a gruesome killing that otherwise might never have been solved. Justice sometimes hangs by a slender thread.

24

A COON OUT OF SEASON

Late one bright fall morning, the officer in charge of the desk of the Bath Village Police Station was startled by a rather tall, heavy-set, good-looking, blond young man who came into his office carrying a shotgun, which the young man laid down on the counter, saying "I just shot a coon out of season."

"You should report that to the game warden, and if you wait a minute I will give you his number," said the officer in charge of the desk.

"I don't mean an animal. I mean a nigger," replied the visitor.

The officer almost jumped out of his seat exclaiming, "I will have to lock you up for that," and took him into custody.

The visitor said his name was Grover C. Ashley. He said he had been living with his wife on the outskirts of the village and that this black man who worked with him in the fields had been "shining up" to his wife. "We got into a row and I shot him in self-defense."

The officer in charge, after locking him up, immediately notified the sheriff who, with his deputies and several officers of the State Police, immediately hurried to the scene of the shooting. They soon found a stake body truck backed up to the back door with a man waiting there scared to death.

The black man, Jacob Simimons, lay dead on the ground near the left front hood of the truck with the top of his head shot off. The coroner and I were summoned and also a photographer who took innumerable pictures of the bloody crime scene.

Investigation showed that the Simmons had been living in the house where Ashley and this lady, who actually was not his wife but his brother's wife, had been living; also that Ashley and the Simmons had had several quarrels about Mrs. Ashley, who was a timid, rather good-looking, mousey type of woman.

Ashley himself had come originally to Bath as a patient in the Veterans' Administration Hospital. He had come from Oklahoma where at one time he had been arrested and convicted for stealing cattle. He was confined in a state penitentiary there. He was also an expert card player and had many card tricks up his sleeve. He had made considerable money among the inmates of the Veterans' Hospital and also with some of the card players around the village. He was known to have a quick temper, drank considerably, gambled heavily, and sometimes not altogether honestly. All in all, he was an unsavory character.

After the last of these rows with Simmons, Ashley had apparently decided to kill him. The night before the shooting, he went to a neighbor's home and borrowed a shotgun under the pretense of going hunting the next morning. In the morning, Simmons was going to move out and that is why he had arranged for the truck to come there to move his goods.

As the truck backed up to the back door, Simmons came tearing out of the house with Ashley in hot pursuit and carrying the shotgun at a ready position trying to get in a position to shoot Simmons. They raced around the truck several times with the driver ducking down on the front seat, not knowing what actually was going to happen.

He finally saw Simmons stealthily walking in a crouched position on one side of the truck, stooped over. Simmons picked up a beer bottle from the ground. Ashley, on the other side of the truck, was in a crouched position with his gun at the "ready," stealthily stalking Simmons.

The poor driver cowered down on his seat in the cab of the truck, terrorized and speechless. As both went by the driver toward the front of the truck, Simmons raised up slightly with the bottle in his hand and seeing Ashley started to throw the bottle at him. At the same time, Ashley raised the gun over the hood of the truck and pulled the trigger of the shotgun, blowing the top of Simmons' head clean off.

Ashley yelled at the driver, "Stay right there until I can go downtown and report this to the police."

Mrs. Ashley, in the meantime, had come out onto the porch and started to cry. She then went back into the house where she stayed until the officers arrived.

Ashley was quickly indicted for first-degree murder and promptly brought to trial. The court assigned two of the best defense trial lawyers in this section, George A. King and John W. Hollis, to defend him. The case came before Honorable William F. Love, an able justice of the Supreme Court from Rochester, New York, who had formerly been an outstanding district attorney of Monroe County, the largest populated county in our nine-county district.

The trial received much publicity due to the fact that Ashley had come to the village police station and turned himself in immediately "for shooting a coon out of season."

The case was very sharply contested along the usual grounds of self-defense and the fact that the shooting was an accident. Ashley claimed that he had not intended to shoot Simmons, that he was merely trying to scare him. Ashley also claimed that Simmons' beer bottle had hit the trigger guard of the gun and jarred it loose, causing it to go off and thus killing Simmons.

Three outstanding events occurred, which made this trial stand out among the many I had in my three years as district attorney.

In this county, we were fortunate to have an outstanding pathologist, Dr. Rudolph J. Shafer, who was head of the county laboratory system. He had taken a great interest in that part of pathology that dealt with autopsies, blood types, and tests of toxins. He had performed an autopsy on Simmons immediately after the shooting. At the trial, he testified about the autopsy on the brain or what was left of it and had with him some of the shotgun pellets that he had removed from the brain and preserved. John Hollis, in questioning him, rather belittled his ability to make competent autopsies, especially those of the brain.

On cross-examination, he asked Dr. Shafer, "Doctor, you don't pretend to know very much about autopsies of the brain, do you?"

"Oh, yes, Mr. Hollis. I have performed quite a few."

"You have? How many would you say? Ten? Twenty-five?"

"Oh yes, many more than that."

"Would you say one hundred?"

"Yes, it would go over a thousand."

"What," yelled Hollis, "there haven't been that many autopsies on the brain in this county in the last one hundred years."

"I didn't perform them here," said Dr. Shafer quietly, "I was the resident pathologist in charge of one of the State Mental Hospitals down on Long Island for a number of years before I moved to this county. And on every patient that died, I was required to perform an operation on his brain and I made studies of the results."

One could sense the telling point that Dr. Shafer had made and how impressed the jury was with this evidence.

Another point that Mr. Hollis questioned Dr. Shafer about was the ability of Simmons to release the bottle after the charge from the gun had hit him, even though he had been in the act of throwing the bottle when the shot was fired. The bottle had been found some ten to twelve feet beyond Ashley and the People claimed that even though Simmons had started to throw the bottle and had been shot during the act of throwing, the momentum would have carried it that far. The defense sought to prove otherwise but without success, and their claim of self-defense depended somewhat on this bottle business, or so they thought.

Prior to the trial, I had talked with Dr. Shafer about the possibilities and importance of this point. He brushed up on his physiology, study of nerve responses, and reaction times to a given stimulus, and also instructed me at length on these subjects. He even lent me several treatises about them, which I "boned up on."

Under cross-examination, Dr. Shafer thwarted every attempt by Mr. Hollis to break down our theory. As a rebuttal witness, Hollis swore in a very able physician from the State Reformatory at Elmira, New York, but alas for Mr. Hollis, that doctor had long since forgotten his elementary physiology and had made no study of nerve reaction times. It was very easy, therefore, to convince him that Dr. Shafer's instructions to me were undoubtedly right and in the end, he wound up as a fine witness for the State.

Once a professional man, such as a doctor, finds that the cross-examiner knows more about some obscure phase of his profession, rarely will he show his ignorance by disagreeing. So, it is and was possible to reinforce our case and belittle the defense. By themselves, little points like this may seem of no importance, but who knows just what convinces a person, especially a juror, of the truth or falsity of statements and events. It's like putting a picture puzzle or a mosaic together, each piece in place brings the whole toward a clearer and quicker finish.

In summation, the many photographs that I had the photographer take at the scene showing the body of the murdered man, the truck, the driver in the cab, the bottle, the house, the porch, and all of the physical surroundings, one item had escaped the attention of the defense attorneys entirely. Against the side of the house, which ran parallel to the truck, about four feet away from it and opposite the hood of the truck, stood standing up, a double-bitted ax. This was within easy reach of the murdered man from where he stood when he was shot, and right near his body where it lay.

Jake Simmons had evidently not seen it when he reached for the bottle, and a bottle is hardly a match for a shotgun in view of the ridiculous unequal claim of self-defense that the defense attorneys were trying to establish. But a double-bitted ax would have given far more power. Had Simmons grabbed it, then the defense would have had a strong argument. I had purposely not said anything about this ax during the trial until summation when defense attorneys had no opportunity to reply. When I pointed that out to the jury, they showed the most intense interest, and you could sense that it was a telling point against the self-defense plea that Mr. King had just made to the jury.

The jury retired after a very impartial and thorough charge by Judge Love on the various degrees of homicide. The judge, by the way, had taken a liking to the fair-haired Oklahoma young man, who had behaved in the court like a perfect gentleman. (I might add, I knew him not to be such, as I had had prior dealings with him in several criminal cases.) Instead of a quick verdict of first-degree murder, which I confidently expected, after a number of hours the jury came back with the verdict of second-degree murder.

I found later that the foreman of the jury, an old friend of mine who had been justice of the peace for many years, had convinced the jury that if they found him guilty of second instead of first-degree murder, there would be no mandatory appeal, and Steuben County would save a lot of money in not having to pay defense attorneys for such an appeal. With this argument, he had swung the other eleven from a first-degree to a second-degree verdict.

In fact, defense attorneys appealed the case and applied for the defendant as a pauper, and the county had to pay the defense expenses anyway. It is often said that a little knowledge of the law is a dangerous thing.

After the verdict, I went into Judge Love's chambers and told him that I thought this fellow was a "bad egg" and that he should give him more than the usual twenty-to-life.

He didn't think so, and while he was telling me that he thought the defendant was a fine-looking young man with a lot of good qualities and that twenty-to-life was enough, a deputy sheriff rushed breathlessly into the chambers to tell the judge that Ashley jumped the sheriff's brother, Deputy Sheriff Hoagland. They were in the automobile as they were about to drive Ashley to jail. He had grabbed Hoagland's revolver, and he and the other deputy had to subdue Ashley with their clubs to keep him from overpowering Deputy Hoagland.

To say that Judge Love was shocked would be putting it mildly. So when Ashley came up for sentencing a week or so later, the judge added five years to the sentence and gave Ashley twenty-five to life.

25
BLACKMAIL

In June 1932 two young fellows named Tony Rucco and Ralph Farrado were apprehended by the Corning Police and charged with blackmail. They were aged about 18 and 28, respectively. They had tried to extort and gain money and property from one Anna Ferns, an elderly widow living in the westerly end of the south side of the city near the Erie Railroad tracks. One day she received a handwritten note, stuck under her door, which read exactly as follows: [i.e. errors have not been corrected]

> "We are adviseing you, to save your life. Only one way. Or we will destroy you and your home. in 24 hours. Because 200 hundred dollars is much better than losing your life. We will tell you were to leave it. Go to the Erie Bridge. And you will find a sign. Says. "Resume Speed." There will be a flat rock write near it on the grown. Leave an envelope with 200 dollars under it. Before Friday Morning. If any one

> else knows. we will take your life just the same so do as we say and keep still if you cant raise 200 dollars do the best you can. But leave a note when you can leave the rest.
>
> We want you to move that Rock from the left Side of the post to the Right Side.
>
> Your friend
Scarhand.
>
> It will not be our fault
> Think it over."

Mrs. Ferns, instead of complying with this threatening note, got in touch with the police who contacted me. We told her to wait because she probably would soon receive another note. Sure enough, a little over a week later she received another note as follows:

> "Your last warning." "Now we will either have the 200 dollars under that Rock. or your life under there" do the same as before. "Move the Rock" Takeing no pitty on you this time.
>
> Scarhand
>
> We want it there by Sunday morning."

Following the advice of Chief of Police Eckess, she placed in an envelope some folded paper covered by a dollar bill. She sealed it, and early that Sunday morning placed it under the rock indicated by "Scarhand."

In the meantime, several city police officers in plain clothes hid themselves in the vicinity. Soon, both of these boys came surreptitiously along, and after making sure that no one was watching, removed the envelope from under the rock. Immediately, the officers closed in on them and arrested them.

They were duly indicted by the next grand jury for violation of Section 856 of the Penal Law against blackmail. My old friend, George A. King, defended them. The case was tried by King and Edwin J. Carpenter before Hon. Edwin S. Brown, County Judge, in the courthouse at Corning. I had gone over the jury list very carefully with Chief of Police Eckess and others. Except for a couple that we did not want, the chief had approved the list.

The morning of the trial, Chief Eckess was detained by some criminal matter in the City Court and did not get to the courthouse until just after I had completed drawing the jury. He rushed up to me at the counsel table and said, "Is it too late to withdraw a juror?"

I told him it was as they had just been sworn in. He moaned, "We are sunk. Juror Number Twelve I now recognize, although I don't remember his name. He is one that I once arrested and convicted for bootlegging."

Much of the defense was based on proof handwriting of one of the defendants. There was no recognized handwriting expert in the Steuben County area. I did not wish to spend the money to hire such a handwriting expert from a larger city because this was a case that I thought was open and shut. But I knew of a man in Elmira who might help.

He was a salesman for the Todd Protectograph Company, which sold check-writing machines to protect merchants and others from forgery. In his business as a salesman, he would show the prospect how easy it was to forge his own name. He would do this very simply by turning a paper upside down and drawing the prospect's signature. Unless you looked very sharply, you couldn't tell the difference between the real signature and the one that he had drawn upside down. He also had made some study of handwriting, especially as to forgery elements.

I talked to him and induced him to start a career as such an expert by testifying for the prosecution.

At trial, when defense counsel objected as to his qualifications, I asked him to step down and obtain the signatures of several of the jurors. I then asked him in front of the jury to imitate their signatures. The jurors showed intense interest, and when he handed the duplicate signatures back to the jurors who had provided theirs, they couldn't tell his imitation from their own signatures. This convinced the jury and the judge that he was qualified as an expert on forgeries and handwriting.

Chief Eckess had obtained samples of the handwriting of each defendant at police headquarters and had had them write some of the exact words that appeared in the two blackmail letters. My witness identified the originals as being written by the same individual who wrote the blackmail letters, which, of course, was one of the defendants, but I have forgotten which one.

The defense swore in my old friend Albert Hamilton. In qualifying himself as a handwriting expert, he gave a very discursive lecture on handwriting and testified that he had made many studies of handwriting specimens, photographed specimens, enlarged them, read all of the standard works on the subject, and had testified on the question of handwriting in many trials, not only in New York State but all over the United States. Then he added, "In one case alone down in Texas, I spent three months and examined four hundred thousand specimens of handwriting in a will contest to determine whether the alleged testator had actually signed the will."

When the defense counsel said, "You may cross-examine," he said parenthetically, "I hope the cross-examination will not be long, as I have an important engagement and must catch the noon train for New York City."

I arose and conducted, perhaps, the best cross-examination I ever made. I said, "Mr. Hamilton, you have this important engagement in New York City and your train leaves in fifteen minutes. If you hurry, you can just catch it." Much to his and defense counsel's amazement, I dismissed him.

When it came to summations, I got a blackboard and wrote on it "400,000 specimens." I then told the jury, "Ordinarily, five minutes a specimen for examination would be a fair and reasonable time." I could tell by their attitude that they seemed to approve. I went on, if you divide five minutes into sixty minutes, that makes twelve specimens an hour. At the rate of ten hours a day, that would be 120 specimens examined each day. Now, Mr. Hamilton said that he examined 400,000 specimens. At 120 a day, that makes 3,330 days, but Mr. Hamilton testified that he spent only three months or ninety days, in Texas. So you can judge yourselves as to how much reliance you can place on the testimony of Mr. Hamilton."

The jury acquitted Rucco but as anticipated, disagreed as to Farrado—eleven for conviction and one for acquittal. The ex-bootlegger had held out just as we anticipated. He told a friend of mine afterward he wouldn't believe the Corning Police under any circumstances.

Farrado was 28 years old and had a prior conviction of forgery for which he had received a suspended sentence, with probation, and then had been arrested for violation of his probation and spent 100 days in Bath jail. Later, when I was about to bring him to trial again, he pleaded guilty to violation of Section 857 of the Penal Law as an attempt to extort money, which was a misdemeanor, and was given a year in Bath jail by Judge Brown.

Thus, another valuable lesson came to light: Exaggeration never pays off, especially on the witness stand.

26

HARDEST JOB

In some respects, a prosecuting attorney can't retain all of his friends like ordinary folks because sometimes friends may get into trouble. The hardest job I ever had happened not because of the work involved or the legal problems, but because the one I had to prosecute was a long-time, boyhood, personal friend of mine. For obvious reasons, I am not naming him. He had been clerk of the city of Corning when I was city attorney. He had continued in that position for a number of years. In cities of this size, the city clerk sells hunting and fishing licenses for the State of New York.

One of the state auditors in examining his books discovered that the city clerk's accounts, which he had rendered to the conservation department of the state, were short. Because of this audit, he had suddenly resigned and had taken off for parts unknown.

On the basis of the audit, I had the grand jury indict him for grand larceny, through embezzlement, and I think also for making a false report to the state. Although it was a sealed indictment, it was pretty generally known that he was wanted by the authorities because the audit had been published in the local press and he had left so suddenly thereafter.

Months had passed when someone told me one day they had seen him when they were visiting Mexico, just across the border from El Paso, Texas. Some weeks after that, his brother came to me and said "Jim (that was not his real name) wants to square himself by coming home and giving himself up if you will recommend leniency for him. His family knows what good friends you two have been, and you ought to do this for him."

I told the brother that I was tremendously sorry for him. I was aware of some of the circumstances leading up to his misstep, and I would like to have helped him. If he were not a public official, I might have been able to do so, but being a public officer, I have always believed "that public office is a public trust and that he would have to face the music." Several other friends of his came to me and tried to get me to reverse my attitude, but I couldn't do it.

A few weeks after that, "Jim" appeared. He came home to Corning voluntarily and gave himself up. He pleaded guilty and when the judge asked me if I had any recommendations, I had to tell him that, in this case, because of his violation of his public trust, I couldn't make any recommendations of leniency.

The judge, therefore, sentenced him to one to three years at Attica State Prison; it almost broke my heart to have to do this. The reason I don't name him is because the younger generation has either not heard of this or has long since forgotten it. He served his time, returned to Corning, became gainfully employed, and reinstated himself as a respected citizen of the community up to the date of his death a few years ago.

27
VAN CISE MURDERS INVESTIGATION

Two rather elderly bachelor brothers, Frank and William Van Cise, lived almost a hermit-like existence on a farm on the Beeman Hollow Road in the town of Erwin near Addison, New York. They raised white leghorn chickens to sell the eggs, and daily, the chickens could be seen scratching the earth of a nearby hillside.

Across a small valley on another road lived a neighbor, Fred Green, who on October 21, 1932, looked across the valley and was surprised not to see any white leghorns on the hillside opposite. For a while, he observed the place without seeing any activity there. Then, filled with curiosity, Green crossed the small valley and climbed the hill.

Just outside the kitchen door, he found one brother lying dead from a bullet wound. The other brother he found inside the house on the floor, also dead from a bullet wound.

In great agitation, he called the sheriff and the State Police who summoned me. We all rushed to the brothers' farmhouse. The weather was unusually cold, and the bodies of both brothers were stiff. Each wore two pairs of overalls, or, as they are also known, dungarees or Levis.

When we drove up the lonely road, it was pitch black. Green had not made his gruesome discovery until dusk. The property consisted of a barn, a chicken coop, and a small, ramshackle house. Frank's body could be seen by the car lights as we pulled into the barnyard. It lay near a cellar passageway. He had been shot in the back, below the right shoulder blade. Another bullet had ripped through his skull, emerging beside the left eye. He had not bled a drop! This led us to believe that he had been shot again as he lay dead on the cold ground.

The front, outside door was partly ajar, being held open by the feet of the dead William. Our flashlights revealed a wooden tub of water sitting on the floor with a pile of dirty clothes, jackets, and overalls beside it. Apparently, William had been doing their wash, as further inspection disclosed clothes hanging on lines near the wood stove, and the clothes were still damp. A lantern on the kitchen table had burned out, indicating that William had been interrupted and then murdered, after dark.

Sheriff Hoagland and I briefly examined the stiff men, and to our astonishment, in the midst of this desolate shack, these hermits had hidden, in the pockets of their inner pair of overalls, $2,000 on Frank's body and $3,600 on William's. The men had wrapped the old bills in oil-cloth packages. We couldn't believe our eyes.

We counted the bills, and the money made a pile as big as two bushel baskets on the rough floor. The bills were of the old, large size type, in denominations of ten and twenty dollars. Some of them were the currency of Abraham Lincoln's time, dated 1865.

William Van Cise, we decided, was the victim of a frontal attack. It appeared as though the bullet tore through his left wrist, plunging into his heart. Quite a clot of blood was pooled around the body. Very little blood had come from the wound where a bullet crashed through his skull above the ears. We decided he, too, must have been shot again as he lay dead on the floor of his home.

It was early in the morning when we finished counting and listing the money, notifying the coroner, and placing a guard at the scene. There being no night depository at the local banks, I took the responsibility for keeping overnight the $6,500 that the murderer or murderers had failed to find.

There had been rumors in the community that these reclusive brothers kept money in their house. As I headed for home, it occurred to me that since the robbers had failed to find any money, somehow word might spread throughout the underworld that I had taken a large amount of money home for the night, for safe-keeping. I parked my car in front of the house, hurried inside with the packages of old bills, and set them on the table near the living room door, while I hung up my hat and coat in the hall.

From my dresser drawer, I took a pearl-handled revolver, which the sheriff had given me, loaded it, and placed the revolver and the bulky packages of money under my pillow. By this time, two things had changed: the money, which had been well-chilled, had now warmed up to the temperature of our house, and my wife had been awakened by the precautionary measures I was taking.

The warmer money, which the Van Cises had been carrying on their persons all these years while tending livestock and chickens, and working their fields, began to "smell to high heaven," which was probably responsible for waking my wife.

"George," she said sleepily, "what smells so bad?"

"Dirty money," I smiled, "$6,500 cash, to be exact."

By this time, she was wide awake and wondered why I couldn't put it in some other room so that we could sleep. Even with the window open, the packages' stench hung in the air and would not dissipate. I told her what we had been called upon to deal with, and we both had very little sleep for the few remaining hours of the night.

For the next two days, Sergeant Burnett and Troopers Lazeroff and Schasel of Painted Post sub-station; Sheriff Stafort, Deputies

Charles Reynolds and Lester Andrews joined me, going over that desolate farmhouse with a fine-tooth comb, searching for clues.

Daylight revealed more than we had been able to make out in the dark by car and flashlight. Coroner W.S. Cobb had directed the removal of the bodies to a local funeral parlor. The Van Cise shack was on the south side of a cleared ravine. On the opposite side of the ravine stood the house of Fred Green, the neighbor who discovered the double murder Friday evening.

Each house was in plain sight of the other, the distance by land being a quarter of a mile. The distance "as the crow flies" was only about half as far. Noises and talking in one yard can be plainly heard in the other. During the Saturday morning investigation, we noticed that we could hear Green's chickens clucking while we were in the Van Cise barnyard.

Further investigation revealed an old-fashioned, single-barreled twelve-gauge shotgun, of the hammer firing type, loaded, and leaning against the shed wall. We theorized that Frank was shot as he made an attempt to get his gun to defend himself from the intruder or intruders. One of the deputies picked up two empty .32 caliber shells, one on the kitchen floor, and the other in the yard.

The most tangible clue was an expensive Stetson hat found near William's body. It was a gray felt hat, six and seven-eighths size, with strands of hair on the sweatband, as though the owner must have had a recent haircut. We later questioned the Endicott haberdasher, whose name was stamped inside the hat, but he declined to attempt to identify the possible owner of the Stetson.

"I must have sold three dozen just like that. How could I possibly recall who bought this particular one?"

Our careful appraisal of the old farm revealed several facets of the hermit brothers' day-to-day existence. The house was stocked with enough provisions to last out the winter: eggs, sacks of flour, potatoes, bread, and other vegetables had been stored away. The livestock were well cared for. All of the 100 chickens had been shut up for the night, the horses had been blanketed, and the three kittens were well-fed.

William Van Cise was reluctant to leave the farm. Most of the time, he walked just to their property line. Frank conducted the business for the pair, taking the wagon into Addison once a week to sell eggs and buy needed supplies. He was last seen in town on Wednesday.

We spent all day Saturday and Sunday in a careful scrutiny of the house and grounds. There was evidence of a struggle. In the living room, one oil lantern had been tipped over, and there was still kerosene on the floor. Fresh dents in the low ceiling looked as though they had been made by the raised butt of a pistol. Both men showed bruises on the head and arms.

By Sunday, over 1,000 persons had visited the scene of the double murder. The sheriff had to assign Deputy Reynolds the task of directing traffic on the narrow, one-way hillside road. How we wished the curious would depart. The troopers strung lines up so that the spectators would not trample, unwittingly, any possible clues. We had already found one spent shell in the yard.

We had assigned two deputies, Lester Andrews and Errol Wheeler, to keep a close watch at the funeral. Nothing new was learned, however, and they left after the minister offered a final prayer and scattered flower petals over the caskets.

William and Frank Van Cise were buried Monday afternoon, on a cold gray October day, leaving behind the probable cause of their murder: $6,529 in hoarded cash. The cash was of little use to them now or during their lives. Robbery, we concluded, was the motive, and the men were killed while attempting to defend their life savings.

A chilly wind blew across the Addison Rural Cemetery as two plain caskets containing the bullet-drilled bodies of the gentle hermits, close partners even in death, were lowered into side-by-side graves.

The days stretched into weeks, and the weeks dissolved into

months, and still, the murderers of the Van Cise brothers remained free. Thinking that more than one person was involved, we tracked down every lead that turned up. The sheriff and I, as well as Sergeant Burnett, became more and more convinced that a gang of thieves had gone to Beeman Hollow that cold October night and had killed the brothers when they resisted the robbery.

Sergeant Burnett and Deputy Andrews made a trip to Blossburg, a small community in Pennsylvania, to question a distant relative by the name of Van Cise. She had written to Sergeant Burnett stating that she knew about the double murder. At first, she seemed quite rational, stating positively that the murderers ran a disorderly house in Elmira.

Sergeant Burnett patiently questioned her, but she could not give the exact location of their illicit business. Then she began to talk in a disconnected fashion, mixing up past and present, and they returned to Corning to report to me that she was not mentally "sound." Inquiries revealed that she had a history of mental illness and had even spent a short period of time in a state hospital.

Concluding that her story was largely a fabrication, a mixture of newspaper accounts and her imagination, we sought out other leads.

A new year arrived and shortly thereafter, a fracas in a roadhouse near Wayland, near the far border of Steuben County, resulted in the turning in of a .32 caliber pistol with notches, five of them, in the handle. Our hopes rose, but tests made on bullets fired with this gun proved that it was not the same one that killed the Van Cise brothers. Four grooves showed on the bullets taken from their bodies. The Wayland gun scored six grooves in each bullet.

Hundreds of people had been interviewed by now, and we had a single, tangible clue, the Stetson hat. All of us agreed that we would not consider the case closed until the perpetrators of the ghastly crime had been brought to justice. There is no statute of limitations on murder.

On Thursday, January 25, 1934, a full year and three months after the slaying of Frank and William Van Cise, the new owner of the Van Cise place, Clarence Button, found a .32 caliber Spanish type pistol in the leaves about a hundred yards from the farmhouse. He related that he and his eleven-year-old son were returning to the house for lunch after cutting some wood. They stopped to rest against an old oak tree and happened to look on the ground where he noticed the handle of the pistol protruding from the leaves.

Feeling certain that it had some connection with the murder case, he hurried to Bath and turned the rusty gun, with a bone handle, over to Sheriff Hoagland. He called me, and Mr. Button told us that the gun was about thirty-five feet from the lane. We surmised that the weapon was thrown aside by a man running down the hill, or it could have been hastily thrown from a fleeing car.

The discovery of the .38 Spanish pistol renewed hope that we would be able to successfully reconstruct the events of October 21, 1932, and then find the guilty men. Both Frank and William Van Cise had been shot down with a .32 caliber pistol, this we knew, but, we reasoned, that the possibility that another man accompanying the killer might have carried the .38 to scare the recluse brothers shouldn't be ruled out.

Once more, the sheriff and his deputies, especially Ray Andrews, who had been assigned to devote a great deal of time to solving the baffling crime, Sergeant Burnett and Trooper Roman Laurence, and I had come tantalizingly close to a solution. But to make an arrest, we needed indisputable evidence to present to a grand jury, so we continued our investigation.

Late in the summer of 1935, Surrogate Judge John C. Wheeler announced that he would seek the post of Supreme Court justice, instead of running for reelection. Immediately, I announced my active candidacy for Judge Wheeler's position as surrogate judge.

In reviewing my record as district attorney of Steuben County, I was faced with the still-to-be-solved Van Cise double-murder case. One of the strangest cases in the annals of the area, it was ever in the back of my mind. The mystery should be solved and the guilty should be brought to justice. In my public announcement that I was seeking the position of surrogate judge, I pointed out my record of convictions and my regret that we had not yet "cracked" the Van Cise case.

I included in the list my accomplishments my goal of making it tough for crooks, so as to make this county a better and safer place in which to live. In my three years of service as district attorney, I had successfully prosecuted over four hundred cases, having been defeated in only eight. Although it is universally admitted that arson is one of the hardest crimes in which to obtain a conviction, I had convicted twenty out of twenty-one defendants.

A rigorous campaign was not needed. I won the Republican Primary, and in our county, this almost amounts to a "win" in the general elections as we are so strongly Republican.

After winning the November election, I was sworn in as surrogate judge on January 1, 1936. However, my interest in the ultimate solution of the Van Cise case did not dim. I notified the lawyer who received the interim appointment by Governor Lehman to fill out my term as district attorney that I would be on call to assist him at a moment's notice should any new developments occur.

The call came ten months later, nearly four years after the fatal crime was committed. District Attorney Michael Cahill directed police in the cities of Corning, Elmira, and Endicott in a surprise round-up of four suspects who were arrested within ten minutes of each other. A fifth man, for whom the police in Endicott carried a warrant, evaded the law and escaped arrest.

The robbery and murder of Frank and William Van Cise occurred on October 21, 1932. The round-up of the gang took place on October 23, 1936. Apprehended were Anthony Mistretta, alias Anthony Bello, of Elmira; James Ross, also known as Onofero Caraci, of Corning; Bertolo Guccia of Endicott; and Anthony Silinonte of the same city.

Silinonte's father, Joseph, had eluded the net and escaped capture at that time.

Warrants charging the defendants with first-degree murder were served by Chief of Police Howard M. Travis of Hornell; Deputy Sheriff Lester Andrews; Chief of Police Leroy Weke of Endicott and his officers; and Chief of Police Eckess of Corning. Sergeant Burnett and Trooper Laurence of the State Police assisted in bringing the men to Corning for questioning.

In declining to disclose the "tip" that he received after taking office in January, District Attorney Cahill said he had been working quietly, obtaining evidence against these men for ten months.

"The killing of the Van Cise brothers was one of the most cold-blooded murders that has ever occurred in this state," Cahill declared. "The murderers were members of one of the most vicious mobs in the gangster underworld. The crime was carefully planned and carefully executed."

In addition to those mentioned, Cahill had sincere praise for Sheriff Fred Cornell, Undersheriff Joseph Bailey, Patrolman Howard Rose, Sergeant Charles Roach and Troopers Compton and Maloney, Motorcycle Policeman Moderhak, and Chief of Police Broughton of Binghamton. All of these lawmen assisted in the quiet investigation leading up to their capture, as well as in the simultaneous apprehension of the four defendants.

A Special Grand Jury was called in December. Winfred Green, the neighbor in Beeman Hollow, told how he discovered the bodies of the Van Cise brothers. Coroner W.S. Cobb testified that Frank and William Van Cise died of .32 caliber bullet wounds. The "clincher" to the evidence against the defendants was the testimony of Trooper Roman J. Laurence. At a hearing, Attorney Costello, representing Bartolo Guccia, sought to have the charges against his client dismissed because Trooper Laurence's testimony was merely hearsay.

Laurence had said, "Anthony Silinonte told me the night we picked them up how he, his father Joseph, and Bartolo Guccia went by car to the Van Cise farm intending to rob them, and that Guccia shot one brother in the house and the other as the three robbers left the home." Laurence stated. "They had heard that the old hermits kept $40,000 to $50,000 in their house. According to young Silinonte, It was a bitter disappointment to come away with only $690."

Laurence also added that Silinonte told him that they went back to Endicott where the stolen money was divided. Silinonte received $230. Judge Wheeler, after taking the testimony under advisement, handed down a decision in favor of Guccia. District Attorney Cahill immediately had Guccia charged with the murder of the other brother, Frank Van Cise.

When the grand jury heard the district attorney's evidence, Cahill had tightened his case against the defendants. He presented the following confession, made by Silinonte, filled with small details he couldn't possibly have known had he not been a participant in the shocking crime. The confession read:

> "Anthony Silinonte, being duly sworn, deposes and says that in October 1932, I and my father and Bartolo Guccia left Endicott in my father's automobile about five or six o'clock at night. We drove to Corning where we stopped at the restaurant of Jim Ross and had some sandwiches and coffee. We remained in the restaurant about a half hour.
>
> "We then got in the car and proceeded toward Addison. It was very dark. When we got about five miles up the road towards Addison, we turned to the right and drove up a dirt road for about a mile. When we got up the road about a mile, we got out of the car, and went into a house, where there were two old men. When we got in the house, my father, Bartolo Guccia, and I demanded that the two old men give us their money. The two old men refused to give us their money and started to fight with us and tried to drive us out of the house.
>
> "Bertolo Guccia got excited and fired a shot into the body of one

of the old men. The old man dropped face down on the floor near the table. We then ran out of the house. The other old man started to follow us, and Bartolo Guccia turned and fired a shot into his body and the old man fell on his face just outside the kitchen door.

"Bartolo Guccia, my father and I then ran out and got in the car. "When the old man in the house fell on the floor, after Bartolo Guccia shot him, Bartolo Guccia reached into the old man's pocket and took out some money.

"I didn't know the names of the two old men shot by Bartolo Guccia until I saw an account of the murder in the papers when I learned their names were Van Cise.

"When we returned to Endicott, Bartolo Guccia gave me $230 as my share of the money he got from the old men.

"This statement is made by me in the presence of Trooper Roman J. Laurence, Chief of Police Howard Travis, of my own free will and without any promises or threats.

"Anthony Silinonte

"Subscribed and sworn to before me this 23rd day of October, 1936.

"Alice F. Adams

"Notary Public, Steuben Co.

"Witnessed by Roman Laurence, Trooper

"Howard M. Travis, Chief of Police, Hornell, N. Y."

By this time, the Van Cise case was fairly bristling with surprises. Thursday, December 31, 1936, brought the news that still another defendant was arrested for the robbery and murder of the two brothers. Gus Alexis, alias Gus Alex or Gus the Greek, was placed under arrest while being treated for a head injury in a New York City hospital. He was charged in the warrant with the slaying of both Frank and William Van Cise.

Deputy Andrews arrested Alexis in New York and brought him back to Steuben County. It was more than mere coincidence that Alexis was the husband of Ida Look's daughter. Ida, you may recall, was questioned at the time of the murder, for she was a cousin of the Van Cise brothers, and she testified that she had seen Frank in Addison three or four days before he was murdered.

Guccia, Silinonte, Ross, Mistretta, and Alexis were all arraigned in Supreme Court on first-degree murder charges for the slaying of the two brothers following the decision handed down by the Special Grand Jury. Representing the People was District Attorney George A. King, the third D.A. to have worked on the Van Cise murder case.

The five defendants in custody pleaded "Not guilty."

King announced that he was calling on the "Scotland Yard" unit of the State Police to assist him in locating the missing member of the gang, Joseph Silinonte. He said he had arranged with Inspector Hoyt of the Batavia Troop to supply aid in bringing in the sixth defendant.

28

VAN CISE MURDERS
FIRST AND SECOND TRIALS

There was a lot of legal "jockeying" for trial arrangements for the Van Cise murders before Justice Wheeler. The outcome was the decision that Anthony Silinonte would have a separate trial because he had made and signed a confession as to how the crime was carried out. The defense attorneys argued that his confession would prejudice the jury against their clients. Judge Wheeler set the trial date of Silinonte and tentatively set a later date for trial for the remaining defendants to be tried before Justice William F. Love.

A bizarre twist in the case took place when D.A. King obtained a court order from County Judge Brown to open the grave of William Van Cise and to remove part of his arm, in order to determine the course of the bullet which took his life. King was empowered to examine the arm from a chemical and physical standpoint and to retain it for the duration of the pending trials of the other five men.

A cold, wintry wind blew across the Addison cemetery as a small group of prosecutor's aides supervised the opening of the grave where the murdered man had lain for four and a half years. Present were Dr. Shafer, county bacteriologist; Dr. Cobb, county coroner; D.A. King, and Deputy Sheriff W. John Semple. A.H. Hamilton, Auburn criminologist and ballistics expert, joined the group later in Addison. The body was reinterred, but the prosecution was granted permission to retain the left arm for the duration of the trials.

The murder trial of Anthony Silinonte proceeded with an inexorable certainty. Introduced into evidence was the old pistol, found near the Van Cise farmhouse, which proved to fit into dents in the ceiling of the living room. They were made, the D.A. positively asserted, when William was battered on the head.

Silinonte's own signed confession was entered. Much to the amazement of the spectators, witnesses were produced who told of seeing Mrs. Ida Look of Corning, a cousin of the murdered brothers, in a car with the defendant, Anthony Silinonte, on the night the grisly crime was committed.

During most of the trial, the twenty-five-year-old defendant seemed unconcerned and read movie magazines. The judge periodically rose from the bench and paced up and down, robes flowing. The defense attorney, North, conducted most of his questioning while seated, rising only to drive home a point. Daily, the crowd of spectators increased, until chairs were brought in to increase the 250-seat capacity of the old Hornell Courthouse.

D.A. King was denied his motion to place into evidence the old Spanish pistol, found by Clarence Button, present occupant of the Van Cise place. A gaunt, raw-boned man in overalls, Mr. Button removed a cud of chewing tobacco from his mouth at the request of Judge Love before giving his testimony. When he had finished, Judge Love conferred with District Attorney King and Defense Attorney North in his chambers.

Then the judge ordered Button's statements stricken from the trial record, stating that "the evidence is not competent on the ground that the occurrence was too remote from the date of the crime." The judge ruled that King had not established the gun's connection with the murder case.

Undersheriff Lester Andrews testified that Anthony Silinonte told him following his arrest that he went to the Van Cise farmhouse with his father and Guccia in his father's Buick touring car. Under questioning, Andrews stated, "Silinonte told me the only part he played in the crime was 'to push the men around,' while his father and Guccia confronted them with guns."

Sergeant Charles G. Burnett related that the defendant, on October 23, 1936, stated that both Joseph Silinonte and Bartolo Guccia fired guns inside the Van Cise house the night of the murder and that one of them threw his gun down a bank as they fled the premises.

Anthony Silinonte stopped looking at his movie magazines long enough to take the witness stand in his own defense. Under Attorney North's careful questioning, the confessed accomplice in the brutal murder and robbery of two harmless, old hermits kept repeating, "Lies, all lies." He said he was threatened with the electric chair, so he signed the confession. He claimed he was told to "sign, sign, sign."

The Endicott haberdasher, Anthony Roach, whose name appeared on the inside band of the gray Stetson hat found at the scene of the crime, testified that he knew both Anthony and Joseph Silinonte. He had sold a Stetson hat to Joseph Silinonte four or five years before, but, he pointed out, he could not remember what color the hat was.

Dr. R.J. Shafer, director of SteubenCounty laboratories, testified that rust scrapings from the "Spanish" gun showed traces of blood, but that he did not test to see if it was human blood. Because Dr. Shafer could not positively state that he found human blood, Judge Love expunged his testimony from the trial record.

Former District Attorney Cahill was called to the stand as a rebuttal witness.

"It was better than 10:00 or 11:00 at night," Cahill related, "when Sergeant Burnett told me Tony wanted to talk to me. I went into the front office where Tony was. I said, 'Do you want to talk about the

Van Cise case?' 'Yes' 'Are you going to tell me the truth about the Van Cise case?' 'Yes.'

"He told me the story. Then I handed him a yellow pad and pencil and asked him to write it. 'No, you write it down,' he said. I proceeded to write it down."

Cahill read what Silinonte had confessed and stated that when he had finished, Silinonte was shown photographs of the dead bodies of the Van Cise brothers. "He covered his eyes and said, 'Take it away,'" Cahill testified.

Silinonte's olive-skinned face began to flush red as Mr. Cahill continued with the story of the confession. "At the conclusion," the witness continued, "Silinonte blurted out, 'I'm an awful rat. My father will shoot me, I'm putting him on the spot. I'm putting Bartolo Guccia on the spot.'

"From my penciled notes, which I read back to Anthony Silinonte, I had a copy typed immediately by my secretary, Mrs. Adams. Then I again read the confession aloud to him, word for word," Cahill related. "After each sentence, I stopped and asked, 'Tony, is that the truth?' He said, 'Yes.' Then he signed it."

D.A. King asked the former district attorney whether anyone threatened Silinonte with the electric chair or ordered him to "Sign, sign, sign."

Cahill denied that any such statements were made in his presence. The same denials were repeated by all those present the night Silinonte confessed: Mrs. Alice Adams, Trooper Roman Laurence, Undersheriff Lester Andrews, Chief Howard Travis, and Sergeant Charles Burnett.

Five days after the beginning of the murder trial of Anthony Silinonte, charged with responsibility for the death of Frank and William Van Cise, which occurred while Silinonte was committing a felony, District Attorney King completed his summation for the People and stated, "The prosecution rests."

Having defined the law as to murder in the first degree, Judge

Love, in his charge to the jury, stated that it was not necessary to prove that Silinonte fired the shot but only that he was a member of a gang that caused the death of William Van Cise while in the act of committing a robbery or felony.

After deliberating for five and a half hours, the men filed back into the jury box. The courtroom was crowded, for word had spread around Hornell that the jury had reached a decision.

The verdict, as announced by Foreman Gerald Hallett, was, "Guilty, as charged, with a recommendation of clemency."

No recommendation of leniency is recognized in New York State law in such a case, and Judge Love, in surprise, asked, "Do you mean the defendant is guilty as charged in the indictment?"

Foreman Hallett firmly stated, "Yes."

Anthony Silinonte was sentenced to die in the electric chair the week of April 26, 1937. The mandatory penalty having been set, Judge Love announced that after two days, Silinonte would be moved from the Steuben County jail to Sing Sing Prison.

Although Joseph Silinonte, father of Anthony, was still at large, the other four were scheduled to be tried together in Corning on April 5, 1937. Two indictments, each charging murder in the first degree, were returned jointly against all six defendants. One, charging the killing of Frank Van Cise, was still sealed.

The other indictment, which was opened, charged the group with the murder of William Van Cise. This was the indictment upon which Anthony Silinonte was tried, found guilty, and sentenced to die in the electric chair. The other four defendants were to be tried for the murder of William Van Cise.

Governor Herbert H. Lehman signed into law a measure, approved by both houses of the New York State Legislature, giving juries the right to recommend life imprisonment instead of the death sentence that had been mandatory in felony murder cases on Monday, March 15, 1937. Although this did not alter the sentence already given to Anthony Silinonte, it might change the sentences to be given to his partners in crime who were awaiting trial. A new option was open to the jury.

Two hundred men were summoned for the jury panel, from which twelve, with two alternates, were to be selected to hear the murder trial of the four in this second trial. The defense put three tables together to accommodate the four defendants and their six attorneys.

D.A. King asked both Mike Cahill and me to assist him in this trial. Also at our table was Michael Fort of the State Police Bureau of Criminal Investigation. Joseph Spagnolia, our key witness, was in the courtroom. In order to testify at the trial, he had been transferred to the Bath jail from Auburn State Prison, where he was serving a term for assault.

The bill of particulars, presented by the prosecution, set forth that Joseph Spagnolia made an affidavit stating that he, James Ross (Onofero Coraci), Bartolo Guccia, Anthony Mistretta, Joseph and Anthony Silinonte, and Gus Alexis were present in Ross' East Market Street restaurant when the defendants conspired to rob the reclusive Van Cise brothers.

The bill set forth that Alexis "aided, abetted, counseled, and planned" the commission of the crime with which he is charged and that his fellow conspirators were the co-defendants. It also charged that Alexis, a relative of the Van Cise brothers, furnished Ross and the others with information as to where the Van Cise brothers lived, their habits, how they carried their money, and the fact that they lived alone. Alexis shared in money taken from the Van Cise brothers, it was claimed on the bill.

Joseph Spagnolia, the prosecution's "star witness," was a former client of D.A. Mike Cahill. He was responsible for pointing the way to a solution to the baffling double murder. Cahill had gone to Auburn

Prison to confer with his client about an appeal while Spagnolia was serving a term there on an assault charge.

In passing, Spagnolia asked, "Did they ever pick up the gang that killed those two old men? They wanted me to come in on that job, but I didn't want any part of it."

When Cahill questioned him further, he related how Mistretta owned a roadhouse with tourist cabins, known as Neptune's Beach, just outside Elmira on the banks of the Chemung River, Mr. Spagnolia had leased the resort from Mistretta and, after renovating it, reopened the place as the Kit Kat Club.

On the basis of Spagnolia's information, and further facts learned from investigating the men he implicated, Cahill was able to direct his dramatic round-up of four of the defendants. Joseph Silinonte must have been out of town or "tipped off" by some friend of the family and was still at large when the Corning trial was in progress.

We always felt that this fact intimidated some of the witnesses, such as Roach, the haberdasher who sold the Stetson hat found at the scene of the crime. His memory might have been clearer had the elder Silinonte been safely in jail instead of in a position to do him harm.

Spagnolia, however, made an excellent witness. Stating that he lived at Neptune Beach in the summer of 1932, he told of several conversations between Mistretta, Ross, Guccia, and Joseph Silinonte. Spagnolia testified that they asked him to join a party to "stick up" two old men living near Addison who, they said, had thirty-five or forty thousand dollars in their possession. He said he refused.

"On October 20, 1932, between nine and nine-thirty in the evening, Guccia, Mistretta, and Joseph Silinonte were at Neptune Beach, and Mistretta said, 'We pulled the Addison job and had to shoot the old men!" Spagnolia stated matter-of-factly on the witness stand.

There was absolute silence in the crowded courtroom as the full impact of his statement struck those present.

Under the district attorney's questioning, Spagnolia related that in 1932 he was employed at the Sears-Roebuck Store in Elmira from February until September and lived at a resort called Neptune Beach, near Fitch's Bridge, on the Caton-Elmira Road. In October, he leased the place from Mistretta and left his job to remodel the establishment.

During 1932, according to his testimony, until September, Bartolo Guccia also lived at Neptune Beach. Then Guccia moved to Endicott. In July 1932, Spagnolia stated, Mistretta told him that two old men near Addison had a considerable amount of money and would be "easy victims for a robbery."

Spagnolia said he talked with Ross at his Corning restaurant, and Ross urged him to join a party in going to the Van Cise place in mid-August 1932. Ross said, "Do you think Tony and Bartolo will go up there?" Spagnolia said that he replied, "Yes, I've talked to them several times, and they're very interested." Ross then said, "Cus Alex, the Greek, doesn't want to wait any longer."

On October 20, 1932, between nine and nine-thirty in the evening, Spagnolia related, Guccia, Mistretta, and Joseph Silinonte came to Neptune Beach. Present at that time were John Kirk, Samuel Sapristone, and Walter Collins, all employees.

Spagnolia testified that he told Mistretta, "Tony, I thought I told you I didn't want these fellows hanging around here." Mistretta replied, "We're only going to be here a few minutes."

Under a biting cross-examination, Defense Attorney Hollis tried to shake his testimony. Spagnolia repeated without change a number of the conversations in which he said the four defendants plotted to rob the Van Cise brothers and later said they killed them.

Despite the confusing questions hurled at him, the witness stuck to his story and maintained his composure. Every seat in the courtroom was taken, and a line of people waited in the corridor, hoping to get a place inside if someone should leave. The cross-examination continued for a grueling two hours, but whether Spagnolia was deceptively calm, or wily, Attorney Hollis failed to get him to change his straightforward account of conspiracy, shooting, and death. Spagnolia also brought to light additional facts that were not discovered in the earlier trial of Anthony Silinonte.

"On about October 29, 1932," Spagnolia continued, "I talked with Jimmy Ross at the Ross Restaurant in Corning. He said, 'Joe, I can't understand how they overlooked $6,000. I think they're holding out some money on me. What am I going to tell Gus Alexis? I can't very well give him $65 or $70 for his end.'

"Early in November of that year," Spagnolia went on, "Guccia returned to Neptune Beach and said, 'Joe, has Jimmy Ross been around here yet? He's supposed to meet me here tonight.'

"After waiting for a time," the witness said, "Guccia declared, 'I don't think Jimmy's coming down. But, will you take this envelope and give it to Jimmy when he comes down?'

"Half an hour later," Spagnolia testified, "Ross arrived, took the envelope, opened it, and counted $65 or $70 in the old, large-size bills." The witness said, "At this point, I changed $50 of the money for a fifty-dollar bill."

Spagnolia continued that Ross said, 'What am I going to do now? I can't go back and tell Gus that's all the money there is. He's liable to squawk." Mistretta said, 'Well, if he does any hollering, tell me and we'll bump him off, too.'"

Following Spagnolia, the prosecutor called to the witness stand John Kirk, the cook, and Walter Collins of Rochester, an entertainer at the Kit Kat Club in 1932. Both swore they saw Anthony Mistretta, Bartolo Guccia, and an older man, later identified by Kirk as Joseph Silinonte, in the Kit Kat Club at about 9:00 p.m. October 20, 1932, the night the Van Cise brothers were murdered.

The D.A. asked Kirk about his employment at the Kit Kat Club. Kirk, testifying in a half-smiling, breezy manner, said he was the cook at the club from October 1932 to January 1933. Kirk, in answer to further questions, stated that on October 19, he went to a secret compartment in the garage to get beer for Spagnolia and saw there a .32 caliber gun, bone-handled, a Spanish type; also a .32 automatic, a

German gun, and two shotguns. The weapons were not there a few days later, he testified.

He was shown a box containing the bone-handled, Spanish gun found at the Van Cise farm and said, "Yes, sir, I saw that gun in there."

Saul Saperstone, a slim, well-dressed, young man, and former bartender at the Kit Kat Club, corroborated Spagnolia's testimony of the presence of Guccia, Mistretta, and Joseph Silinonte at the Kit Kat Club on the evening of October 20, 1932. He, too, confirmed the fact there was a "secret trap" in the garage on the premises, in which there were a number of guns. One, in particular, he had noticed because it was unusual, "about eight or nine inches long, bone-handled, with the words 'made in Spain' on it."

Saperstone also testified that Anthony Mistretta, not Joseph Spagnolia, used the garage.

The first woman witness to be called was Shirley Converse, formerly a waitress at the Kit Kat Club.

D.A. King asked, "How long have you known the defendant Mistretta?"

Mrs. Converse replied, "Fifteen years."

"When did you meet the defendant Guccia?" King asked.

"July or August, 1932."

"Was there ever a time when you saw more than one of them at the club at the same time?"

"I saw three of them there, Mistretta, Guccia, and Ross," Mrs. Converse replied.

"What were they doing?"

"Talking in the dance hall."

King pressed, "When?"

"Sometime in July."

"State whether there was any other time when you saw them together."

"Yes, in August, the last part of August," she answered.

Mrs. Converse further testified that she had seen the men

together when Guccia invited her to go "along for the ride" while he delivered some alcohol to Ross at his Corning restaurant. "Again, about mid-September," she stated, "he asked me if I wanted to go to Utica with him. I went with him and he got a load of alcohol."

Prohibition was still in force in the summer of 1932, so obtaining and supplying alcohol was illegal. Attorney Hollis was aroused by Shirley Converse's repeated references, and he moved immediately for a mistrial, claiming that the district attorney was introducing unnecessary prejudicial material. Judge Love denied the motion but sternly reprimanded the district attorney for straying "pretty far from the points at issue."

During the trip to Utica, Mrs. Converse stated, she saw a gun in Guccia's car. "It was black, short, flat, and black," she testified. King asked her if she had ever seen this gun before, and she said she had seen Guccia shoot tin cans on a post at Neptune's Beach.

"When the gun fired, what did you notice?" King asked.

"The bullets came out each time the gun was fired."

King sought to clarify the witness' response. "You mean the shells?"

Converse replied, "Yes, the shells."

The prosecution had provided testimony of Coroner Cobb that William Van Cise was shot and killed by a .32 Colt revolver, an automatic pistol, which ejects the cartridge after each discharge.

D.A. King called another woman to the witness stand, Mrs. Harry J. Spotts. She testified that on the night of the double murder, she saw Mrs. Ida Look of Corning, mother-in-law of Gus Alexis, and niece of the Van Cise brothers. Mrs. Look, she stated, positively, was riding through Corning in a "dark-colored coupe" driven by Anthony Silinonte. This happened, she declared, at 9:30 p.m., October 20, 1932.

With Mrs. Look facing her, sitting in the first row of spectators, Mrs. Spotts of 121 East Pulteney Street, forthrightly declared that Mrs. Look was indeed a passenger in a car driven by Anthony Silinonte that swung the corner of Bridge and Pulteney Street so fast as nearly to run down Mrs. Spotts and her daughter, Louella, seventeen.

She related that she did not see the car until it was about six feet from her, that she jumped out of the way, and she saw Anthony Silinonte so clearly that "that picture will be in my mind as long as I live."

"You couldn't possibly be mistaken?" Mr. Hollis asked.

"No, sir," she replied in a firm voice.

The reason she remembered the exact time and date was that it was her husband's regular bowling night, so he had the car. She had taken her daughter to the neighborhood theater, The Plaza, and it was a single feature. They went to the first show. While walking the few blocks to her home, they were nearly run down by Silinonte's coupe. This occurred at the main "four corners" of Corning's north side, and there is a street light on each corner.

Remembering how Anthony Aurigemma, an investigator for the National Board of Fire Underwriters, helped me obtain inside information from the arson gang three years before, which was instrumental in placing them behind bars, I called on him once again to see if, in this five-year-old case, he could learn anything new from the defendants who were being kept in jail. His extensive knowledge of various Italian dialects was invaluable in understanding their conversation when they spoke to each other in their native tongue, to keep their remarks secret from the jail attendants.

At my request, as assistant to D.A. King, Aurigemma was arrested and committed as a vagrant to the Steuben County Jail at Bath. He was placed in Cell No. 5 while Anthony Mistretta and Bartolo Guccia were in Cells No. 7 and No. 9.

On direct examination, Aurigemma testified that the previous Sunday afternoon, about 3:00, he was with Mistretta and Guccia in the corridor of the jail. He stated that Mistretta was reading a paper and said to Guccia, "That dirty ___ even described your suit." He said Guccia replied, "You know yourself I did not have that suit on that night we do the job."

He testified that Mistretta admonished, "If you not get excited, you not shoot that man. Remember how cool I was? If you were cool like I was, you would not shoot that man."

Again on Monday night, Aurigemma stated that he was standing on his bed in the jail cell and heard Mistretta and Guccia talking. He said Mistretta told Guccia, "When you take the stand, deny everything. If others say I answer the telephone at the Kit Kat Club, you say, "It was my wife calling me up. Ross is going to say the same thing."

Aurigemma's testimony, as a plant in the county jail, caused a buzz of excitement in the courtroom. Previous testimony was largely a repetition of that given during the Hornell trial of Anthony Silinonte. Aurigemma's corroboration of the guilt of the defendants from their recent conversation was devastating to the defendant's case. The prosecution received a counter-blast when their surprise witness was held in contempt of court for refusing to give his home address.

When he finally stated his address, with extreme reluctance, he noted that it was the first time in years of investigating that he had been required to tell in court where he lived. As an undercover man for the Board of Fire Underwriters, he stated, he is supposed to keep his residence secret, for his own safety.

A long recess followed, and Judge Love returned to announce that he was dismissing the charge against Gus Alexis on the ground that there was no evidence to connect the defendant, Alexis, with a conspiracy. "The only competent evidence against him," the judge continued, "relates to the division of the money and the rule of evidence pertaining to conspiracy does not apply to him because he was not placed in the conspiracy until after the crime."

The defense based its case on the testimony of Mrs. Anthony Mistretta, who provided an alibi for her husband. She swore that, although her husband retained a key to his private entrance to Neptune Beach, he was in Binghamton on the night of the murder. In fact, she maintained, he was in Binghamton from October 19th to October 22nd, 1932.

Defense Attorney Lewis Mosher, counsel for Mistretta, called other members of Mrs. Mistretta's family, who testified that Mistretta stayed with them the days she had indicated. Mrs. Mistretta led the family witnesses, stating that she, her husband, Anthony, Mrs. Mistretta's father and mother, her brother and his wife, went to Neptune Beach, Mistretta's resort, Tuesday, returning to Binghamton the next day for the anniversary party of her brother William and his wife. She said Anthony accompanied them and stayed in Binghamton with her until they returned to Elmira for the opening of the Kit Kat Club, successor to Neptune Beach, just starting up under the management of prosecution witness Joseph Spagnolia.

One of the most colorful of the defense witnesses was Joseph Mazzola of Rochester, the man described by Spagnolia in his testimony as a "racketeer." Slender, slightly bald, with a mile-a-minute flow of words, in a strong Latin accent, Mazzola took the witness stand wearing his topcoat, carrying his hat. He punctuated his testimony with flourishes of the hat, and after testifying for half an hour, he pulled off his coat and called for a glass of water.

Spagnolia had testified that Mistretta and Guccia invited Mazzola to join them in a "stick-up" of the Van Cise brothers and that the Rochester man declined. On the stand, Mazzola denied that the matter was even mentioned to him.

On cross-examination, he stated that the only business that brought him to Neptune Beach was the game machines that he had stored in one of the cottages there, about twenty-eight of them. He said he had hoped to place them at Spagnolia's Kit Kat Club.

Bartolo Guccia took the witness stand in his own defense. He was questioned by his attorney, Costello, who asked him to describe his career. In a strong accent, with a husky, almost hoarse voice, Guccia said he would be forty-five in December. He related that he came to the United States from Italy when he was eighteen.

He got a job in Endicott working for a sole leather tannery connected with the Endicott-Johnson Shoe Company. From there, he went to Brooklyn where he was hired as a stevedore, loading freight on the docks. He met and married his wife, who spoke only her native Italian. She testified through an interpreter.

They moved back to Endicott where he "conducted a poolroom." Later he opened a saloon, which he sold to open a taxi business. His cousin, Anthony Mistretta, sold him his first car.

Then his testimony came closer to the facts of the case. Attorney Costello asked him if he had spent any time at Neptune Beach, which became the Kit Kat Club. Early in 1932, he said, he came to Neptune Beach to work for Anthony Mistretta, then proprietor.

Asked what his job was, he replied, "Bartend, sell liquor, wine, beer." He said the liquor was always kept in a locked "trap" in the garage. After the opening of the Kit Kat Club, he stated, he worked for Joe Spagnolia. Asked about the cars there, he answered, "Mistretta had two cars, a Chevy coupe and a Cadillac." Once, he reported, Mistretta took his wife back to Binghamton in a Packard.

On cross-examination, I asked Guccia to describe the secret "trap." Guccia replied that it was about a foot and a half wide and extended the length of the side of the garage, like a false wall. Guccia stubbornly denied all allegations of previous witnesses that he shot and killed William Van Cise or that he went to the Van Cise farm in 1932 with Mistretta and the Silinontes, even that he owned a gun, or had ever seen one at Neptune Beach.

I asked Guccia about Aurigemma's testimony, the "plant" sent to the Steuben County Jail, during the trial. Aurigemma had said that Guccia and Mistretta had talked over the Van Cise crime, and their part in it, but Guccia denied this. He said that he had been aware from the beginning that the man was a "plant" and declared he never spoke to Aurigemma except to refuse to play a game of casino with him.

He dodged my questions as to his whereabouts the night the

gruesome crime was committed. He said he couldn't remember where he was on the night of October 20, 1932.

Yes, he admitted, he owned and carried a handgun. He said he carried it in the car when he was transporting alcohol. "Transporting alcohol" was a polite expression for bootlegging.

Guccia claimed that some years before he had had an argument with Joe Silinonte over "money matters" and that the two families were not on friendly terms and hadn't spoken to each other since. ,

Having been indicted for the two murders, Joseph Silinonte was still a fugitive. So far, he had managed to elude the law, but they were still searching for him.

Next to take the witness stand was defendant Anthony Mistretta. He admitted he had a gun, just one, a shotgun he used for hunting. He testified that the only cars he owned in 1932 were a Packard and an Oldsmobile.

Asked about Anthony Aurigemma, the "plant" who testified that he heard incriminating conversations at the jail between Mistretta and Guccia, Mistretta said, "I knew all the time the man was a Stool pigeon, so I had no conversation with him or in his presence about the Van Cise case or the trial."

James Ross, also known as Onofero Corraci, who owned a restaurant in Corning, denied ever knowing Guccia until they were picked up in 1936. He also denied ever knowing Joseph Silinonte, still being sought for the double murder. He admitted having been convicted once for violation of the Prohibition Act and once for reckless driving.

Mistretta testified that he knew Shirley Converse, a waitress at the Kit Kat Club. "She lived in Room 5 over the bathhouse," he stated.

"Isn't it a fact that you had her in your car several times?" D.A. King asked.

Mistretta shook his head, "No."

"Isn't it a fact that you told Shirley Converse that you were afraid that Joe Spagnolia might squawk on you about killing the old men?" shot out King.

Judge Love sustained Hollis' objection, so the witness had plenty of time to regain his composure." On October 2nd, Mistretta testified, his wife went away from Neptune Beach, unexpectedly."

"Was it because of Shirley Converse?"

"I don't know."

"Did you know where she was going?"

"No, sir," Mistretta answered. "I went to bed and I no see my wife."

The next day, he related, he found out through Spagnolia that she had gone to Washington to stay with a brother-in-law. He drove to Washington, made up with her, and brought her home.

Attorney Costello, defending Guccia, gave a skillful summation. He termed Joseph Spagnolia's detailed story "the most fantastic and inconceivable story I ever heard on the witness stand. He is the most skilled liar you men ever met in your lives," he proclaimed.

"What have they got to send these men to the electric chair? Just one other piece of evidence," intoned Costello, referring to Aurigemma's testimony about the conversations made in the Steuben County Jail.

Costello flatly stated it was highly improbable that men on trial for their lives, especially if they were guilty, would converse about the case in jail before strangers. He failed to point out that they thought they were the only ones who understood their Italian, and Aurigemma was an expert on all of the dialects of Italian, a fact they were not aware of. So they would mistakenly think that no one present in the jail could understand their conversation, and thus be more inclined to talk freely.

"Mistretta's alibi, placing him in Binghamton on October 20, 1932, the night Spagnolia swore he saw him at Neptune Beach, destroys Spagnolia's evidence against all the defendants."

The case was due to go to the jury on a Friday morning. The four defense attorneys had finished their summations just before the close of court on Thursday. During the next twenty-four hours, something occurred that completely reversed the attitude of the jurors, and consequently, their verdict.

Harry Sanford, a farmer in the town of Thurston, was serving as Juror Number 3. He reported to Judge Love on Saturday morning that he was tending his cows Thursday night and that three men, hats pulled down over their faces, stopped him abruptly by stepping out of the shadows by the barn door. They told him that "he would be rewarded by seeking acquittal and that harm would come to him if he voted for conviction."

In fear for his life, he asked Judge Love to relieve him from jury duty immediately. The judge conferred with all of the attorneys in his chambers for several hours. When court convened, Judge Love announced that Juror Sanford had been excused and that he would be replaced by Morris Williams of Woodhull, one of the two alternate jurors who had heard the entire case in the event that an emergency occurred. This would save the costly expense of a re-trial.

The jury went out immediately after lunch and returned at 4:00 to request that Joseph Spagnolia's testimony be read to them by the court clerk. They listened attentively despite the fact that the reading took eight hours. At its conclusion, the jury retired to rooms at the Baron Steuben Hotel for the night.

All day Saturday, the jury was still out. They caused a stir when they returned to the courtroom in the afternoon. The attorneys for the prosecution and the attorneys for the defense thought that the jurors had reached a verdict. But hope waned when the foreman asked to have the clerk read from the court record the testimony of Aurigemma, the jail "plant," who worked for the National Board of Fire Underwriters as a secret investigator. They listened again, intently, then retired to the jury room.

As Saturday's day of deliberations produced no verdict, the jury took up the double murder case of the Beeman Hollow hermits on Monday. Finally, after thirty-four hours of deliberating, the jury returned to the courtroom. Foreman Spear was asked if they had reached a verdict. He replied, "Your Honor, after careful consideration of all of the evidence, the jury finds itself unable to agree. Continued deliberation would be useless."

Judge Love thanked the jury and dismissed them. Then he asked the prosecution if they intended to retry the defendants. Receiving an affirmative reply, he set a date for the new trial.

The defense counsel moved again for a change of venue.

Judge Love set the motion down for argument in Corning.

29
VAN CISE MURDERS
THIRD TRIAL

Reports had circulated around Corning that the jury in the second trial had stood ten to two for conviction. One thing was obvious. The three men who intimidated Juror Number 3, Harry Stanford, succeeded in frightening the other jurors, for it was no secret why Sanford was excused after hearing twenty-two days of testimony.

Even before the change of venue motion was argued in Corning, Justice Love announced in an Associated Press dispatch, dated Canandaigua, May 19, 1937, that he had dismissed the charges against Gus Alexis of felony murder, conspiracy to commit robbery, and murder of Frank Van Cise. His dismissal cited "Insufficient evidence" as grounds for dismissal.

The change of venue request was granted, and the trial of the three remaining defendants, Guccia, Mistretta, and Ross, alias Coraci, was placed on the court calendar in Canandaigua, Ontario County, for October 11, 1937.

An interesting event occurred at this time. Women were granted the right to serve on jury duty, but Canandaigua authorities planned to assemble an all-male jury because a final explanation of the new law had not yet been received.

The course of the new trial was similar to the Corning murder trial. The prosecutor called Fred Green, the neighbor, who discovered the frozen bodies of the Beeman Hollow hermits. He again described the circumstances and was unable to state the exact date when he thought he had heard two shots and a car driving off the week of the gruesome murders.

Undersheriff Andrews told of his finding the now-famous Stetson hat and the two empty shells, practically the only physical evidence unearthed in exhaustive searching of the premises. The Spanish pistol, found later near the farmhouse by the new owner of the remote rural property, was not yet allowed to be introduced into evidence.

Andrews described his discovery of $2,396 on Frank's body and $3,644 on William's body, both being in oilcloth packets, in the pockets of an inner pair of overalls. The men were wearing two pairs of overalls at the time they were struck down.

Again, Joseph Spagnolia, proprietor of the Kit Kat Club, recited his account of the meetings between Guccia, Mistretta, and Ross, planning to rob the Van Cise brothers, and that they later returned to his nightclub the night of the double murder and told how in the course of the "stick-up" at the Van Cise place, they had to shoot the old men.

Saul Saperstone, cashier and waiter at the Kit Kat Club, identified the bone-handled pistol, found on the Van Cise farm more than a year after Frank and William were killed. He positively stated that Mistretta had shown him the gun at the club in October 1932, the month the murders were committed.

Still, the pistol was not admitted into evidence. True, it was not the murder weapon, but the men had been beaten with a gun, and it had been used to intimidate them.

On the night of the murder, Saperstone testified, he saw Guccia, Mistretta, and another man he didn't recognize get out of a dark coupe in the driveway of the club, and "they came right into the kitchen." He pointed out Guccia and Mistretta in the courtroom. The third man was unshaven, hair uncombed, and wore coarse trousers and an odd coat, according to Saperstone. He said they spoke in Italian, so he did not know what they were talking about.

Sergeant Burnett testified briefly as to receiving the gun, found by Button. Once more, the People were denied the right to place the pistol in evidence.

John Kirk, club chef, became the State's third witness to place Mistretta and Guccia at the Kit Kat Club at about 9:00, October 20, 1932. According to Kirk, "They got out of the car in front of the kitchen window, coming into the kitchen itself. An older man in particular, shabby, unshaven, no hat, was along with Guccia and Mistretta. I told them Joe didn't want them hanging around. They said they were going in a few minutes. Joe Spagnolia came soon after and told them he didn't want them hanging around. Then the phone rang. Mistretta answered. Early in October," he continued, "Mistretta told me to be careful when I went into the trap in the garage or the guns might fall and go off and shoot me.

"In the trap, I saw a shotgun against the wall, a black .32 automatic, a .38 old Spanish-type pistol, and a blackjack. Had the Spanish pistol in my hand, and found the name Alamo Ranger, made in Spain. It had a bone handle, was blue steel, and an odd sort of hammer."

"Yes," he stated positively, identifying the gun found by Button at the Van Cise farm.

Sergeant Burnett was recalled by the district attorney in another attempt to have the Spanish revolver admitted as evidence, but was again balked. The four shells from the cylinder of the gun were denied as evidence, as was the Stetson hat. Anthony Aurigemma, the undercover man who posed as a prisoner in the Steuben County Jail during the Corning trial, repeated his testimony of having overheard Mistretta tell Guccia in Italian, "If you never get excited and shoot that man, we not be arrested and Anthony Silinonte never make that confession."

Anthony Silinonte was still on "Death Row" at Sing Sing, having been sentenced to die for the murder of Frank Van Cise. This was a felony murder conviction, for Anthony explained that he was just the driver when the crime was committed.

In a dramatic appeal for a missing witness to appear, D.A. King rose in the courtroom to ask Mrs. Shirley Converse, Kit Kat Club waitress and a witness at the Corning trial, to take the stand. Mrs. Converse had been in court at the opening of the Canandaigua trial but was mysteriously missing on the day that the D.A. repeated his call for her to come forward to be sworn in as a witness.

Finally, the prosecution rested its case, having been unable to locate Shirley Converse. All of the defense attorneys moved for dismissal of the case against the defendants. Judge Love denied their motion, and the defense opened its case.

Much to the amazement of those present, the first witness for the defense was Shirley Converse. Although a subpoenaed State's witness who failed to show up for her testimony, she walked uncertainly to the witness stand and was sworn in.

Then Mrs. Converse stated that her testimony in the Corning trial was false, given only at the insistence of Joseph Spagnolia on the promise that she would be well paid. On cross-examination, she admitted that at no prior time did she tell the D.A. or any other officer that her testimony was false.

At the Corning trial, she had stated that she saw a gun in Guccia's car, had seen other guns in "the trap" at the Kit Kat Club, that Mistretta told her he went to Addison with other men, "and pulled that job." All this she now said was false.

The following defense witness was Gus Alex, alias Gus the Greek, or Constantine Alexopolis. He was formerly a defendant himself. He testified that he had never conspired with Ross to rob Frank and William Van Cise, cousins of his mother-in-law.

Anthony Mistretta, alias Tony Bello, took the stand on his own behalf. On direct examination by his attorney, Lewis Mosher,

Mistretta stated he knew Jimmy Ross and had even roomed with him in Corning while searching for a business place to open. Finally, he found and operated Neptune Beach in Elmira. He also revealed that Bartolo Guccia was a "second or third cousin on his mother's side."

As his alibi witness had testified, he was with relatives attending an anniversary party, which lasted several days, in Binghamton, at the time the hermit brothers were robbed, beaten, and murdered.

Attorney Mosher: "Did you come to the Kit Kat Club on October 20, 1932, around 9:00 with Guccia and Silinonte and tell Joseph Spagnolia of having pulled the Addison job and having to shoot the two men?"

Mistretta: "No."

Mosher: "Did you tell Spagnolia that Guccia got excited and shot and that you also fired?"

Mistretta: "No."

Mosher: "Did you say that Joe Silinonte complained that the Van Cise brothers had pushed his boy, Tony, around?"

Mistretta: "No."

Mosher: "Did you ever receive any proceeds from the robbery?"

Mistretta: "No."

The next defendant to be sworn in was Bartolo Guccia, "trigger man," according to Anthony Silinonte's confession. He admitted a conviction for carrying a concealed weapon. Also, he admitted owning a Smith revolver, for which he said he had a permit. Another gun he had, he said, he purchased from a Pete Como for fifteen dollars.

Further questioning revealed that he had carried still another revolver in his car, which Shirley Converse had mentioned, but later repudiated as a fabrication. The pistol he kept in the car was stolen, according to Guccia's testimony. He said that when he was arrested, all of his guns were confiscated.

On direct examination, Guccia admitted that he had been in a partnership with Joseph Silinonte, operating a "speakeasy" for "about six weeks, after which we had an argument over money, and I sold out and started bootlegging myself!" He also admitted three convictions for Prohibition Law offenses—possession of liquor.

Attorney Costello questioned Guccia thoroughly: "Did you ever have any talk at Neptune Beach or anywhere with Ross, Mistretta, and Joe Spagnolia about robbing two old men who had a lot of money; did you ever kill anybody in your life; did you ever rob anybody?"

Guccia replied with an emphatic, "No, sir."

When court convened, Thursday, November 4, 1937, Judge Love issued an ultimatum. He firmly declared that the testimony must be completed that day, even if an evening session was required. At about noon-time, Mistretta complained of feeling very ill. During the noon recess, he was taken to a local physician. He was instructed to try to continue during the afternoon, but as court continued nearly half an hour over the usual closing time, Mistretta groaned, doubled over, and appeared to be deathly pale. Observers attributed his trouble to ulcers for which he had been treated for several years.

The State produced a surprise rebuttal witness who had not testified at the two previous trials, Mortimer Root of Addison. He related that he had been at Neptune Beach, and while sitting at the bar drinking his glass of beer, he saw Mistretta take a bone-handled revolver out of a drawer and load it. He continued, "I got scared, and I got out of there in a hurry."

D.A. King then showed Root Exhibit #30, the Spanish-made pistol, which he had finally succeeded in getting admitted into evidence. Root didn't hesitate to identify it as either the pistol he saw Mistretta load at the bar or "one exactly like it."

Under cross-examination by Attorney Hollis, Root was asked, "Have you a gun?"

Root replied matter-of-factly, "Yes, right here with me, on my hip!" A gasp was heard in the silence that followed this statement.

Root went on, "It's a .38 caliber Colt. Have been carrying it over a period of several years. Yes, I've got a permit. Want to see it?" He reached into his pocket and produced a permit issued March 4, 1937.

Root stated that he hadn't seen the Spanish gun from the time Mistretta showed it to him at the Kit Kat Club until it was shown to him by the district attorney on the witness stand. He further claimed he had never mentioned seeing it on Mistretta because "I didn't want to get mixed up in this affair."

In rapid-fire fashion, Hollis asked, "You are prejudiced against the Italian race, aren't you?" "You married an Italian girl and you are now divorced; you were stabbed by an Italian, too, weren't you? That is the reason you are carrying the gun, isn't it?"

Root claimed no particular prejudice against anyone, and added, "Yes, I'm carrying this gun for my own protection."

John Spagnolia, brother of Joseph, the State's star witness, denied that he had told former D.A. Cahill he knew something about the case, but did not dare to testify because the mob would kill him; denied telling Trooper Forte in Hornell that he had been offered a large sum of money to leave town or at least not testify, and denied having lived at Neptune Beach or any other place with Shirley Converse, saying only, "Yes, I see her occasionally, but that is all."

Summations began, as Judge Love assigned each lawyer one hour. Attorney Costello, counsel for Guccia, declared Spagnolia's story had no other corroboration than the stories of his own kin and "pals."

Actually, Mistretta's alibi was substantiated by his many relatives, and Guccia offered no alibi at all. Ross's attorney said that a conspiracy had not been proven and that even a felony murder didn't stand up, for the prosecution had failed to prove that indeed a robbery had occurred at all.

Late as the hour was, the case finally went to the jury following Judge Love's charge. They deliberated for six hours.

A verdict of "Not Guilty" was returned to a tense courtroom in the early morning hours. This ended the charges against Anthony Mistretta, alias Tony Bello, James Ross, alias Onofero Coracci, and Bartolo Guccia for the murder of William Van Cise.

When the verdict was brought in at 3:00 in the morning, the

defendants, stolid throughout the trial, retained their composure. Their wives were less self-contained.

Mrs. Ross gasped, "My God."

Mrs. Guccia nearly fainted.

Defense attorneys moved to have the second indictment against their clients dismissed for the murder of Frank Van Cise. Judge Love set bail of $5,000 for each, and bonds were provided.

After having spent a year in prison, the men were allowed to go home.

Anthony Silinonte was still in the death house at Sing Sing Prison. According to his own confession, he was just the driver of the car that took two of the three men, who had just been set free, to Beeman Hollow that fateful night to rob the hermit brothers. His conviction had been appealed, and the State Court of Appeals had not yet handed down its decision.

D.A. King felt morally certain that the Canandaigua verdict was a miscarriage of justice. Unable to have the case heard by any other judge than Love, even with the change of venue, he had little opportunity for a fresh interpretation of the facts. Even the arguments for dismissal of the second murder indictment would in all probability be heard by Judge Love.

Once more, this unusual case took a strange turn. A general alarm was broadcast throughout the state and surrounding areas for Joseph Spagnolia, Auburn Prison convict, who had been kept in Steuben County Jail at Bath during the two murder trials in order to testify as the State's star witness.

A week after the acquittal of the three defendants, whom Spagnolia had accused of plotting to rob the aged Van Cise brothers, Spagnolia escaped from jail. According to the reconstruction of the jailbreak by Sheriff Bailey, he slipped from the third-floor cell, crept through the darkness, down a stairway in the middle section of the jail, and passed out of doors through the jail laundry.

Deputy Sheriff Andrews explained that Spagnolia had been in a highly nervous state ever since the completion of the Canandaigua trial when the three defendants were acquitted. "He had about eighteen months left to serve in Auburn Prison, and he was afraid he would be murdered if sent back to prison." When he made his daring escape, Spagnolia was dressed in the same street clothing he had been wearing for trial.

The State Court of Appeals then affirmed Silinonte's conviction and refused to grant him a new trial. The State Court of Appeals was to set the date of execution.

Unless Governor Lehman intervened with executive clemency, or unless the State Prison Board should examine Silinonte and find him insane, he was doomed. The governor could commute his sentence, on the grounds of insanity, in which case he would be committed to an institution for the criminally insane until sanity returned when the sentence would then be carried out.

Coincidentally with fixing the week of January 3, 1938, for execution for Silinonte, the Court of Appeals announced that a commission had been appointed to test his sanity. After having been sworn in by the chairman of the commission, Silinonte declared that there were "50,000 girls in his pillow." He told the members of the commission that he was worth four-hundred and seventy-five billion dollars. One of the doctors stated that "Silinonte is the victim of a physical ailment as the result of which his condition is not good."

Governor Lehman announced that the commission had found Silinonte insane, and therefore he ordered that he be removed from Death Row to the Dannemora State Hospital for insane convicts, "there to remain until restored to his right mind." The governor's announcement came one month before Silinonte was scheduled to die in the electric chair.

Ross, Guccia, and Mistretta were still out on bail, pending their appeal of Judge Love's denial of their motion to dismiss the indictment for the murder of Frank Van Cise. They argued that they had already been tried twice, the first trial resulting in disagreement, and the second in acquittal.

During the first trial in Corning, two men threatened a juror just before the case was to go to the jury. During the Canandaigua trial, the prosecutor's witness, Shirley Converse, mysteriously disappeared and failed to take the stand for the prosecution. A week later, she just as mysteriously appeared, only to testify for the defense, and to claim that her Corning trial was "all lies." She claimed that she had perjured herself at the first murder trial.

D.A. King asked me to help him oppose the defense dismissal claims before the Appellate Division in Rochester. I was eager to appear for the People, as I, too, was convinced that there had been a miscarriage of justice when the Canandaigua verdict was reached.

Before we made our trip to Rochester to argue for retention of the murder indictment against Ross, Guccia, and Mistretta, Mrs. Converse was arrested on a first-degree perjury charge. At the Corning murder trial, she testified that she saw Guccia shooting at Neptune Beach with "a small, flat, black gun." She swore, under oath, that Mistretta told her he went to Addison with other men and "pulled that job." But at the second murder trial in Canandaigua, Mrs. Converse switched to the side of the defense, denying statements made in Corning, and the three men were consequently acquitted on the charge of murder of William Van Cise.

Following her arrest on the perjury charge, Mrs. Converse was released on $1,000 bail. The bail was posted by Frank Mistretta, brother of the defendant, Anthony. Bail was accepted, despite the objection of D.A. King that this was improper in view of the relationship of the two men to the case in question and to each other.

Arraigned before Judge Brown in Bath County Court in March, Mrs. Converse, represented by Attorneys Costello, Hollis, and Becker, entered a plea of not guilty to the charge of perjury! A bit of legal maneuvering produced a stay in her trial instead of quick justice.

Judge Brown found it unavoidable to issue an order directing the D.A. to show cause in the April term of Supreme Court in Geneseo why defense counsel should not be permitted to inspect the minutes of the grand jury that indicted Mrs. Converse and why the first-degree perjury should not be dismissed.

As you may have guessed, Judge Love was sitting at the Geneseo April term of court. He directed King to produce for his perusal the grand jury minutes and requested both sides to submit briefs.

The following week, Mrs. Converse changed her plea to one of guilty of perjury, first degree, on which Judge Love suspended sentence. She left the courtroom a free woman.

"It is clear to the court," Judge Love stated, "that you were the victim of what in the Court's opinion was a worse crime of subornation of perjury which I fully believe was committed here."

D.A. King and I appeared before Judge Love in Rochester on a cold day in December to argue for the retention of the indictment of Guccia, Mistretta, and Ross for the murder of Frank Van Cise. Still at large was Joseph Spagnolia, after six successful years of eluding the law.

Sometimes the law seems slow. Even Hamlet bemoaned "the law's delays in action." Then a startling announcement was made over the Associated Press.

This time, the wait seemed unnecessarily long. Joseph Spagnolia, the State's star witness who escaped from Bath Jail rather than go back to Auburn Prison to face the retribution of friends and relatives of the defendants who were already in that same prison, had been arrested in Florida.

This one news story may have nudged Judge Love a bit, for his decision on our arguments made four months earlier was soon forthcoming. Interest in the still unresolved Van Cise murder case mounted daily, as more information reached Steuben County. The district attorney felt that with his star witness once more available for testifying, he could bring the defendants to trial for Frank Van Cise's murder.

Joe Spagnolia waived extradition and was escorted from St. Petersburg to Auburn Prison by two members of the State Department of Correction. Prison doors had clanged shut at Auburn when District Attorney King received this brief message by wire: "Spagnolia arrived this institution, 4:30 p.m., April 17, 1939. Joseph M. Brophy, Warden."

The next turn in this remarkable case was a statement issued by the county's only woman lawyer, Mrs. Mary Karr Jackson, now representing Joseph Spagnolia, a convict-witness who was seeking a pardon from Auburn Prison.

"A dead man's voice will speak from the grave in an appeal to release this man," Mrs. Jackson stated. Spagnolia maintains that he was promised a pardon if he would tell all he knew about the Van Cise case. Mrs. Jackson was referring to the late District Attorney Michael H. Cahill, the prosecutor who "cracked" the case, staged a whirlwind round-up in three cities, and arrested five men for plotting and participating in the Beeman Hollow killing of Frank and William Van Cise.

In still another surprising development, Joseph Silinonte, long a fugitive from justice, was arrested without resistance in Brooklyn. He had been working as a stevedore on the docks. District Attorney King revealed that he had continually kept Mrs. Silinonte's house there under surveillance since King had become D.A. His patience paid off, for the father of convicted Anthony Silinonte was brought back to Steuben County to stand trial for the murder of the Van Cise brothers.

By now, early December 1940, eight years after the grisly crime in the remote Beeman Hollow, it looked as though the fourth district attorney would represent the People against the killers of Frank and William Van Cise. George King had been elected to the office of county judge in November and was to be sworn in in January 1941. This meant that Governor Lehman would make an interim appointment, which he did. He selected Attorney Holland B. Williams of Corning to fulfill the unexpired term of District Attorney King.

Supreme Court Justice John C. Wheeler granted a change of venue to Ontario County for the murder trial of Joseph Silinonte upon the motion of his attorney, John Hollis. Hollis argued that the wide publicity given to the three Van Cise trials of five other defendants named in the same indictments with Joseph Silinonte had created prejudice in this county.

In response, George King, assisting Holland Williams, declared that Silinonte remained in hiding while his son, Anthony, was tried and convicted of murder, even sentenced to die in the electric chair in the Van Cise case. He declared that the People were ready for immediate trial and said it would be much more economical to hold the trial in Steuben County.

Judge Wheeler, pointing out that Justice Clyde W. Knapp, after study of the case, had granted a change of venue for the third Van Cise trial, stated he would follow the same course and grant the change. "Justice N.D. Lapham opens a term of court in Canandaigua in early February, and so far as I know, the Silinonte case could be moved to the calendar for that term," Wheeler declared.

Before the murder case could come to trial again, court convened in Bath, and the returned escapee, Joseph Spagnolia, was tried. He pleaded guilty to a charge of jailbreaking and was placed on five years probation. Neatly dressed in a double-breasted, brown suit and gray-striped tie, Spagnolia looked suave enough to prompt one of the legal secretaries to exclaim, "He's the handsomest man I ever saw!"

Although Judge Love heard arguments for the retention or dismissal of the murder indictment for the murder of Frank Van Cise, November 20, 1937; he had still reserved decision at the time that Joseph Spagnolia was picked up in Florida, in April 1939. Mistretta, Ross, and Guccia had been out on bail all that time.

It wasn't until after the apprehension of Joseph Silinonte, a fugitive from justice these many years, that Judge Love finally handed down his decision on the motions argued before him in 1937. On Friday, February 28, 1941, he dismissed all murder charges against Ross, Mistretta, and Guccia, as well as against Joseph Silinonte, for the murder of Frank Van Cise, and for the murder of both aged brothers, against Silinonte, Sr.! This despite the fact that I had shown laboratory proof that the very Stetson hat found at the scene of the gruesome crime contained hairs on the inside hatband that matched hairs from the head of Joseph Silinonte.

Still, Judge Love acquitted all defendants, with the exception of young Silinonte who was sent to Dannamora for the criminally insane following his sentence to die in the electric chair for aiding those who were set free! The Supreme Court Justice's reason: "Lack of sufficient evidence!"

This sweeping decision, which was four years in the making, was announced on a Friday, although Judge Love had already left Rochester for New York City, and thence to Florida, with Mrs. Love. This trip came to light when it was discovered that in order to officially release Joseph Silinonte, Love's signature was required. It took a while to locate the elusive justice.

Meanwhile, Sheriff Benjamin Balcom, concerned because of what he felt to be a miscarriage of justice, held a warrant, issued by the United States Office of Immigration in Buffalo, for the arrest of one Joseph Silinonte. This long-sought fugitive from justice, recently set free by Judge Love, had actually entered this country illegally. He was an alien. Balcom felt that it would be a small crumb of justice if he could succeed in having this man deported.

After releasing him from Bath Jail, the sheriff served him, and Silinonte appeared in Rochester to answer the charges. He was let out on $1,000 bail pending disposition of his case.

This seemed to be the end of the road for the celebrated Van Cise double murder case, still listed as one of the most baffling to have ever occurred in our county, and still listed as officially "unsolved" despite the conviction of one of the six defendants. The road had led through fruitless investigation, sudden revelation, three trials, four district attorneys, six defense lawyers, a perjured witness, and a threatened juror.

It was an interesting postscript to the entire proceeding when I chanced to read the list of Mafia bosses who were guests at the Apalachin meeting at the home of Joseph Barbara, where state troopers staged a spectacular round-up, catching some big Mafia fish, in the net. This was the famous raid near Binghamton in 1967.

From the page jumped the name of one of the "guests," Bartolo Guccia.

THE END

www.ingramcontent.com/pod-product-compliance
Lightning Source LLC
Chambersburg PA
CBHW022043160426
43209CB00002B/51